OTHER KINDS OF TREASON

OTHER KINDS OF TREASON

TED ALLBEURY

NEW ENGLISH LIBRARY

British Library Cataloguing in Publication Data
Allbeury, Ted *1917*–
    Other kinds of treason.
    I. Title
    823.914 [F]

ISBN 0-450-49598-1

This collection first published 1990

Published by New English Library,
a hardcover imprint of Hodder and Stoughton,
a division of Hodder and Stoughton Ltd,
Mill Road, Dunton Green, Sevenoaks, Kent TN13 2YA
Editorial Office: 47 Bedford Square, London WC1B 3DP

Typeset by Hewer Text Composition Services, Edinburgh
Printed & Bound in Great Britain by Butler & Tanner Ltd, Frome, Somerset

To Nigel and Fran Dickson
with much love

Contents

INTRODUCTION

I didn't start writing until I was fifty-five. I had never thought about being a writer nor particularly wanted to be one. My start didn't come out of sudden inspiration but out of an entirely negative situation. Something happened in my private life that depressed me deeply. Enough to end up taking those green pills to get through the day and the purple ones to get through the night. I gave up work and the world and retreated into the lethargy and despair that go with depression. For some unknown reason I wrote four chapters of a book. Its central thrust was based on my experiences as an intelligence officer in Occupied Germany. The four chapters were shown by somebody to a literary agent who phoned me a few days later to say that he had sold my book to St Martin's Press in New York and was selling it to a British publisher the next day. Would I get a move on and finish it? As all would-be writers know, it's not this easy to get published – but that's how it happened. It sure was a cure for my depression because the pretty Polish girl from the typing agency who came to type the manuscript is still around. We got married.

Since then I've written thirty-one novels, some short stories and a number of radio plays and serials for the BBC. And, naturally, you learn a few things in the course of all that writing. When I first started writing I worked out a plot and bolted on the characters, but by about book number seven I realised that what I liked writing about most was the people. Their problems and their relationships. It also dawned on me that nobody was stopping me from writing any way I wanted to. So I start now with the people and the plot allows them to work out their destinies. I think that

1

I now write novels that just happen to have espionage as their setting.

I am often asked what makes a writer, and how to set about being one. The second question is the easier to answer. Buy yourself a W. H. Smith jumbo pad and pencil – and start writing. There are books on how to write. Some good, some not so good. Then read a lot, especially the kind of books you would like to write. But when it comes to what makes a writer, I don't know the answer. It's like playing the piano by ear. You don't know how you do it.

However, I can tell you what doesn't make a writer. It's not formal education. My headmaster told my Grandma that I was on the dustheap of the school and would be on the dustheap of life. I was pleased to be guest of honour a few years back at the school's bicentenary. More importantly, it's obviously never too late to start. If I can start from scratch at age fifty-five so can anyone else. I strongly recommend that you write while you still have a full-time job. I did, and this meant writing until two in the morning and all day Saturdays and Sundays. I'm a strong believer that anyone can do anything if they want to do it enough. And it's the last part that is the test. Do you really want to do it enough?

Obviously I get asked if it helps that I was an Intelligence officer myself. It does help in some ways, but just knowing what happens doesn't mean that you can write about it well enough to interest readers. Authenticity doesn't come from knowing which way the safety catch goes on a Walther PPK. It comes from the everyday feelings of what it was like when you were being trained and what it felt like on your first job.

Perhaps the most important thing that you learn from doing the job is that whether you are SIS, CIA or KGB you are all men, recruited in much the same way and trained in much the same way. And doing the same kind of work. This means that you end up with more in common with your opposite numbers than you have with your own civilian population.

There is a kind of hypocrisy, particularly in this country, that surrounds the Security and Intelligence services. Even when they catch a spy or a traitor, the shout goes up – 'Why didn't they catch him sooner?' Every country has its own Intelligence services and certainly ours and the Americans' do a good job of work. Sometimes things have to be done that are not "kosher" but if the nation wants protection from foreigners' interference these things have to be done. The men who work in these services are, admittedly, specially trained to do their jobs. But they are perfectly ordinary men with mortgages, families and responsibilities. Like the rest of us they can be lonely and perhaps cynical, but on the whole they behave like you and I would behave doing their job. And what I have said about men applies equally to the women in the services.

It seems a terrible thing to say, but for young men like me from the less posh suburbs of Birmingham the war was our university. A broadening of our vision and the exercise of our minds and imaginations far beyond what would have happened if we had not been involved. Irrational though it may be, I still feel an affinity with those men and women who were in the services rather than those who were not. Shakespeare's Henry V's speech at Agincourt about "gentlemen in England now a-bed" is still valid for me. And that means that I have little sympathy for those, mainly Brits, who write non-fiction books purporting to prove that our Intelligence services are being run by traitors and double-agents. And even less sympathy for those who publish the names of serving officers so that their lives are endangered.

Ted Allbeury
Lamberhurst
Kent

THE THREE ANGELS

A lot of people seemed to find it surprising, even incredible, that a man could bring up two girls, but it had seemed simple enough to me in the doing. The nanny had stayed on after Helen died, I was reasonably well-off and I worked at home. And I never tried to be a mother as well as a father. It had meant dodging a few issues that were essentially feminine but between Nanny Freeman and school they seemed to have filled in the gaps all right. To me it had seemed all quite simple and straightforward. I loved my two daughters and taking care of them was, in my fortunate circumstances, a pleasure not a burden.

Victoria is thirteen. Very pretty. Blonde and leggy, with a temperament and character very like Helen's. Pauline is dark and beautiful, calm and slightly aloof. At eighteen she seemed to have more common sense than I had myself. No doubts about herself or how life should be lived. She seemed to have inner strength rather than the bounce and enthusiasm of young Tory. I sometimes had to look away when one of her gestures was too like Helen to be ignored.

I had found that while time didn't heal all wounds, it was possible to keep the memories of Helen under control for most of the time. But there were odd things – a song, a place, Chanel No. 5, *Le Figaro* on a news stand or a smell of bluebells in a wood – and she was there as if she had never been away. Sometimes, late at night when I was tired and perhaps uncertain about some film-script that I was writing, my low spirits could dissolve into depression at the thoughts that came surging back. So real that my mind started going over camera angles, lighting and dialogue as if it were some script that I was working on.

If my memories could have been only of that lovely happy-go-lucky girl and our days of wine and roses, they would have been welcome. But, inevitably, my thoughts were of the two years of deterioration and those last months of doomed failure when love and caring were not enough. But I had kept all that from the girls. It had meant letting Helen become a vague background figure. Not mentioning her birthday, our wedding anniversary or even the date of her death.

The past closes quickly behind young children and I had done my best to keep the door tightly closed. When they were older and more mature, perhaps I could tell them how it had been. Unfair to the dead but beneficial for the living. I was never sure that this was the right way to deal with the problem and sometimes I had the dread that some day I would be proved wrong and a lot of birds would be flying back home to roost.

The birds started flying home the following Christmas when Pauline was unpacking from her first term at college. I was sitting with her in her room, chatting as she put her clothes in drawers and her books on the shelves. She had not responded very enthusiastically as we talked and finally she sat on her bed facing me, her big eyes looking at me intently.

'Tell me about Moma.'

'What about her, sweetie?'

'Everything.'

'Is something worrying you?'

'Yes.'

'What? Tell me.'

'Was Moma a drunk?'

'What on earth made you ask that?'

'A reporter from a newspaper phoned me at college and said he wanted to interview me. He came down and showed me some old newspaper cuttings about Moma. He said he was doing a piece about forgotten heroines of World War Two. He said he'd contacted you and you'd refused to see him.' She paused. 'One of the newspaper cuttings was about her death. It implied that she'd died of drink and drugs.'

'What did you say to him – the reporter?'

'The same as you. I told him to go to hell.'

'Reporters are used to that. I can't imagine he just went.'

She smiled wryly. 'I opened the window and asked somebody

to find one of the college servants as I was being pestered by a man.' She shrugged. 'He left before one of the porters arrived.'

'Have you told Tory about this?'

'No.'

'Why not?'

'I wanted to talk to you first.'

'Was that because you thought that the newspaper cuttings were true?'

'I'm not sure.'

'How about we leave it until tomorrow and I'll talk to you both about it?'

'Whatever you want.'

'Let's do that. We'll go out for lunch and come back home and talk.' I paused. 'Meanwhile, I want to say something to you. Don't ever judge people by their appearance or what other people say about them. Other people could be gossips or liars, mistaken or even intentionally mischievous. Your Moma was a beautiful, brave, honest and . . . well, I'll tell you tomorrow. Let's all have a glass of champagne to celebrate us being back together again.'

I tried to sleep that night but failed, and about 2 a.m. I got up and went to my study with a cup of tea. I turned on the gas fire and sat in my old leather chair. I may be a film-script writer but this time I was in the wrong film. People were tired of hearing about the war and the girls were no exception. They knew more about the Battle of Hastings than they did about World War Two. And that had suited me fine. But there was no way I could give them a fair picture of what happened with Helen without explaining what the war had been like in Special Operations Executive. And inevitably my mind went back to the Dordogne.

The small cottage and workshop was on the outskirts of Brantôme. Perched on a small hill so that anyone approaching by car or on foot could be seen long before they arrived.

There were no lights on that night, just a candle in a bottle as she put on the headphones. It was a Mark III suitcase transceiver and she was working on the "blue" frequency band. I watched her check the meter and then switch to transmission, her finger already resting on the black cap of the micro key.

She moved the candle with her free hand as she tapped out our call-sign, so that she could read the message pad more easily. She turned the switch to receive and waited for London to respond.

After they had come through she turned the switch to transmit and tapped out the groups of five letters.

I remembered standing up and walking to the window. I could see the glow of François' cigarette as he stood watching the approach road. It was two months after D-Day and things were much tougher now. The Gestapo and the Sicherheitsdienst were lashing out ruthlessly at all the Resistance networks. Being in the Unoccupied Zone was no longer any protection. It seemed crazy that, as the Allied armies fought their way into Europe, we were facing the near annihilation of groups that had two or more years of resistance experience.

I turned to look at Helen. She was still taking down coded traffic from London and I looked at my watch. She'd been on air for nearly ten minutes and that was too long. There were Gestapo teams with direction-finding vans that the Germans had brought up from Bordeaux and they were now operating from Angoulême, roaming the countryside at night listening for unauthorised radio transmissions. In the right weather conditions we could transmit to London in daylight but the darkness gave us a stronger signal path.

As I watched she switched the set off, took off the headphones and shook her blonde hair, running the long slim fingers of one hand through it as she checked the switches on the radio before putting it back in its wooden box.

It was midnight before I had decoded the messages from London. And it was almost 1 a.m. when I told the girls to call it a day. When I was away the three of them slept in the attic and a casual inspection of the cottage would indicate that only one person lived there. The three of them would disperse to other locations as soon as it was light.

Afterwards I felt guilty that I hadn't said goodbye to any of them before I left on my cycle. I spoke for a few moments to Paul-Henri, who had taken over from François, and then I pedalled off down the slope of the hill and turned on to the road to Brantôme, heading for my room at the back of the café. There was nothing special in the traffic from London that night and I slept until ten that morning.

I dressed and shaved in a leisurely way and had just lit a cigarette when I heard the knock on the door. The emergency code knock. Forty-four in Morse. Four dots and a dash repeated. It was Aristide, the café owner. Not one of the network but an active sympathiser. His face was white and his whole body was shaking as I opened the door and let him in.

8

He was almost too disturbed to give me the news. He had to keep pausing to get his breath back. The Germans had raided the cottage at dawn and four other locations during the night. Seventeen of the network had been arrested. He said that the three girls had been taken to Angoulême and the others to Périgueux.

The next week was a nightmare of hurried, desperate journeys trying to check how much of the network was left intact. There were few survivors. Certainly not enough experienced people left to constitute a network. I released them all from their obligations and was aware that one of them was perhaps a traitor. The Gestapo sweep had been too thorough and too accurate for it to be the result of just surveillance. Somebody had definitely betrayed us.

I made my way to Brive where there was a radio-operator used by a network that operated out of Cahors. I needed to let London know that we had been betrayed and wiped out. And it was then that I learned that Helen had not been caught in the raid on the cottage. She had escaped but had been picked up fifteen days later in a shop in Angoulême. That was all I could find out about her at that time. London sent in a Lysander for me a week later and I spent the last months of the war at SOE's headquarters in Baker Street.

And for some inexplicable reason, thinking of Baker Street made me think of the club. The Special Forces Club. They'd get a feel of the atmosphere of the Resistance. And as if that had solved all the problems, I was suddenly tired and I slept through until morning in the leather armchair.

It was years since I had been to the club. There were too many memories there. Too many reminders. But Helen and I had lunched there most Saturdays. Sometimes with a baby in a carry-cot asleep under the bar counter. Carefully watched over by Albert, the barman.

Going there would maybe bring the two worlds together. The Special Forces Club members mainly consisted of old SOE and SAS people with a few from the wilder areas of military intelligence. And if I was lucky it would provide me with some inspiration on how to tell the girls what had happened. I wanted them to have the right picture of their mother. Sooner or later they would hear some snide, weasel version and they had to be armed to confront it. Two months of dying doesn't represent a whole life.

I booked a table for the three of us for lunch that day.

*

The three of us sat at a table by the tall windows with a bottle of the club Bordeaux, the girls sipping gingerly and, I suspected, wishing that it was a Coke. When Michael signalled to us that our lunch was ready we walked over to the dining-room.

We were just by the door when Vi came into the bar and, seeing me, she waved and walked over to us slowly, prodding the carpet with her stick and breathless when she got to us.

'Harry. My dear. How lovely to see you here. We've all missed you. How are you?'

'I'm fine, Vi, thank you. Let me introduce you to my daughters. This is Victoria and this is Pauline.'

She looked at them each in turn and then back at me. Her voice trembled as she said quietly, 'They're so lovely, Harry. She would have loved them so much.'

I saw her try to blink the tears away but she had to put up her hand to smooth her cheeks.

There was a slightly awkward silence and then she said, 'It all seems a long, long time ago, doesn't it? She's so like her, Harry.'

She turned and headed unsteadily for the bar.

We were eating our crème caramel when Pauline said, 'By the way, who was the old bag?'

'What old bag?'

'The one with the blue rinse hair and too much rouge who spoke to you by the door.'

It would have seemed to me a harsh commentary in any circumstances but in that place at that time it was like a physical blow. I felt a quick flush of anger. And that was unfair. The comment may have been flippant and unkind but it was no more than that. It was made in ignorance.

'Her name's Vi. Vi Harty. She's a club member. She knew your mother very well.'

'Are you cross with me?'

'Why do you say that?'

'You said "your mother" – you usually say "Moma".'

'No, I'm not cross with you. Drink up your coffees and we'll get on our way.'

I'd paid the bill and we went down the stairs slowly, the girls not even glancing at the photographs on the wall. Photographs of the heroes and heroines of the Resistance in France, Holland and Norway.

Halfway down, I stopped them in front of the three photographs grouped together. The photographs of three pretty young women. One smiling, the other two looking rather solemn.

I pointed at the photographs. 'Do you know who they are?'

The girls looked at the photographs but without any real interest. They exchanged glances and shrugs as they said 'No' together.

'You should recognise the one on the right. Have a good look.'

Victoria said slowly as she looked at the photograph, 'They're all very pretty. The one on the right reminds me of someone.'

'Go on.'

'In fact she's very like Pauline,' she said slowly. 'The same eyes, all big and bedroomy, and the same mouth.' She turned quickly. 'It's Moma, isn't it? It's our Moma.'

I nodded, smiling. 'Yes. That's Moma. She was about four years older than Pauline is now when that was taken. She'd just finished her training course.'

'It says underneath – *Les Trois Anges* – the three angels – why that?'

'It was a joke. They were very close friends. All on the same training course. All three of them were highly rated except for discipline. They were all rather naughty so far as the army's rules and regulations were concerned. That's why they got the nickname, because they always looked so surprised and angelic when they were confronted with their misdeeds.'

'What sort of misdeeds, Daddy?'

'Nothing very bad. They were just a bit wild.'

'Who's the one in the centre?'

'She was Pauline. You were named after her. She was caught by the Gestapo and died in a concentration camp. Ravensbrück. A lot of SOE girls died there.'

'And the one on the left? The smashing blonde?'

'She was a special friend of Moma's.'

'What's her name?'

'Well, her name then was Violette Daudet. I'll tell you about her some time.'

I'd cast the baited hook deliberately for Victoria who could never wait for anything. She rose so easily.

'Tell us now or you'll just forget.'

'Let's get home and I'll tell you about the three of them.'

I settled them down in my study and looked from one to the other.

'So, what do we talk about?'

It was Tory who rose to the bait, as usual.

'Tell us about Moma and how she was when you first knew her. Where did you meet her?'

'She was on an SOE course at Beaulieu. I had gone there to give a talk about how a network was run in the field. I noticed how pretty she was and I also noticed that she yawned twice while I was saying my piece.'

'Did you chat her up?'

Pauline laughed. 'I can't imagine Daddy chatting up pretty girls.'

'Why not? I bet he did, didn't you, Daddy?'

I smiled. 'Let's leave it that I didn't chat your mother up. I was also going to take back a new radio operator. They gave me a file marked "Helen McNay" and I read through it several times and then told them that I didn't want her. She wasn't suitable.'

'That was Moma, I bet. Why wasn't she suitable?'

'Well, she was top of the list for almost everything. Coding, radio, driving, parachuting, shooting – everything. But she'd been put on a charge three times in three months.'

'What's "put on a charge"?'

'Being taken in front of the Commanding Officer for doing something you shouldn't do.'

I saw that they were both interested now. 'What had she done?'

'Well, the first charge was insolence to an officer instructor. And she'd said some very rude things about him. But he wasn't very popular and she was just reprimanded. The second time it was disobedience on active service. And that's pretty serious. She'd been told how to do something with the team she was in charge of. She completely ignored the order and did it her own way. She got docked two days' pay which was the minimum they could do. She'd admitted what she had done and pointed out that her way was quicker. It was, but it was still a bit naughty. The third charge was that on ten different occasions she had used one of His Majesty's vehicles and petrol for unauthorised journeys. I don't think that it helped that all the journeys were to a night-club in Mayfair – the Embassy Club.' I smiled. 'She was very fond of dancing and having a good time.'

'Did they find you somebody else?'

'No. They insisted that I at least gave her an interview. As you know, she was very pretty – and very charming. She convinced me that if I took her as my radio operator there would be no indiscipline and no wild behaviour.'

'What sort of things did you do in SOE? Were you spies?'

'Oh, no. Nothing like that. We blew up bridges and roads and electricity pylons. General sabotage. And we organised French resisters. Got them weapons and explosives and trained them on how to use them.'

'But girls just did radio stuff?'

'No. Some girls were couriers. That was very dangerous work. And some carried out sabotage missions the same as the men.'

'How did she get into SOE?'

'She spoke fluent French because she was brought up in France. Somebody contacted her and she volunteered. We were all volunteers.'

'And she actually shot with guns and actually parachuted?'

'Yes. Bren guns and pistols and a parachute course at Ringway. Where Manchester airport is now.'

'She must have been very brave.'

'Yes, she was.'

'Did she mess about when she was your radio operator?'

'No. Never. She was first-class in every way. A good operator and she was as disciplined as anybody else in the networks.'

'Did you fall in love with her while you were in France?'

'I liked her a lot, admired her but there wasn't the time or the . . .' I shrugged, '. . . the peace to love someone. At night we were exhausted, just longing for the chance to close our eyes and sleep. I was away a lot too. It was a big area to cover. We had seven sections in the various towns. I had to visit them to keep up morale. We didn't see much of one another in those last few months.' I paused. 'She saw Pauline from time to time and one or two other girls from SOE.'

Victoria sat with her head resting on her knees and her sister sat in the armchair, her head turned to look at the fire burning in the grate.

It was Victoria who said, 'Go on. When did you fall in love with each other and where did you get married?'

'We got married about a year after the war ended.' I smiled. 'We were married in a hospital chapel.'

'Had you been wounded or something?'

'No. It was Moma who was in hospital.'

'Was she wounded?'

'No. But Moma had been very ill. It took a long time to get her better again.'

'What was the matter with her?'

'She had TB, tuberculosis. Nobody gets it any more but in those days they didn't have all our modern drugs and treatments. People were very frightened by it. They didn't even like to say the word out loud. They just said somebody had a weak chest, or an infected chest. It made people who got it very depressed. And it was very contagious so you had to be in an isolation hospital and kept away from other people.'

'So how did you get to see her?'

'I pulled some strings. Old SOE strings. But I was a civilian by then.'

'How did she get to be so ill?'

'The three girls in that group of photographs were all in my network. Pauline was a courier. Violette was an explosives and sabotage expert. And Moma was the radio operator. In the autumn of 1944 the network was wiped out by the Gestapo. Pauline and Violette were taken to Angoulême for interrogation. Moma got away but had to abandon her radio and code-books. I was in Brantôme that day, so they didn't get me.

'We never found out what happened to Pauline in the prison. But she was sent to a concentration camp called Ravensbrück. A lot of captured SOE girls were sent there. Most of them – including Pauline – died in the ovens there. We found that out from the camp records after the war was over.'

'Don't get upset, Daddy.' It was Pauline who interrupted.

I was aware that my voice was unsteady as I went on. 'When a network was taken there were always certain people the Germans most wanted. The leader of the network, that was me, the radio-operator, that was Moma, and the couriers. Obviously, if they could be persuaded to talk it gave the Gestapo tremendous advantages in countering resistance.

'So – they hadn't got me and they hadn't got Moma. And that meant working on Pauline and Violette. We know that both of them were tortured and it's just possible that one of them succumbed to the pain. Probably Pauline. We know it wasn't Violette because she survived.'

'Would she tell you, even if she had?'

'We didn't really need to ask her. She was tortured and abused. Sadly enough, the evidence was on her body. They used pliers to pull off her toe-nails and finger-nails and she was never able to walk properly again. Even today she is in constant pain. She wouldn't have needed to go through all that if she'd talked.' I paused. 'And she was Moma's best friend. And that meant a lot in those days. It was no disgrace, by the way, to talk. All we were expected to do was hold out for two days so that the rest of the network could disperse.

'Anyway, by luck or some other means the Germans eventually picked up Moma. She and Violette were removed for further interrogation to Fresnes prison in Paris. There was no record that they had been moved there and it was a month after Paris had been liberated before we discovered where they were.

'I got them back to England. Violette was engaged to an Englishman – she was French – and they married that Christmas.'

'What about Moma?'

'She was half-starved and she'd had a very rough time but she seemed to recover quite quickly. We saw a lot of one another and we became engaged. I'd got my first film assignment and we started looking for a flat.

'Then, quite by chance, we met Violette at the food shop at Harrods. They hadn't met since the war and I left them talking to one another.

'That evening we were due to have dinner together at the Royal Court but she didn't turn up. I phoned but there was no answer so I went round to her room in Kensington. She was there and I could see that she was very distressed.

'It was the first time that she had learned about what happened to Pauline and Violette. She was convinced that just as the injuries that Violette had suffered were to save her – Moma – from the Germans, so was Pauline's death. She was in such a bad state that I phoned for her doctor. She was taken to hospital that night and the next day they diagnosed that she had TB.

'She was in hospital for almost a year. We married just before she was due out. I thought it might cheer her up. When she came out it seemed to have worked. She was free from the TB and full of energy. She got a job at an antique bookshop. Then Pauline came along and Moma gave up the job. She seemed very happy. Just like when I first knew her. Eventually there was Victoria and we took on Nanny Freeman.

'We went out quite a lot. Theatres, concerts and dinner parties and all seemed so well. We never talked about the war and I avoided seeing Violette and her husband. I didn't want anything to remind her of the old days. We went to the club most Saturdays but that was because she wanted to.

'Then one night we were at a dinner party and somehow the talk got on to SOE, and some idiot man said that SOE had just spent their time sunbathing on the Riviera. Moma threw a glass of wine in his face and walked out. I went with her.

'I told her the man was just an ignorant fool and to ignore what he said. She looked at me strangely and said, "Maybe he was a fool, and maybe he was ignorant, but in a way he was right." I asked her why she thought that and she said very quietly, "Nobody cares what we did, Harry. We wasted our lives. It was all a waste of time. A ghastly game." She started to cry and then she said, "Poor Pauline, poor Violette, and nobody cares."

'I talked to her for hours that night but it didn't have much effect. She was like that for a week and then suddenly one evening it all seemed to go. She was laughing and happy-go-lucky again. I was terribly relieved.

'It was like that for about four months. Then I had a phone call from Violette. She wanted to see me. She told me she was terribly worried about Moma. That she was drinking heavily and was taking drugs. All sorts of drugs. I could hardly believe it but she said that our doctor knew about it.

'I went to see him. He was very cagey but he confirmed what Violette had told me. I asked him what had caused it and I can remember even now what he said: "Your wife's got a guilt complex a mile wide." I asked him why she should feel guilty and he shrugged and said, "One friend dead because she protected her, and another disfigured for life in the same cause. Enough to make anyone guilty, surely?" He made it seem like being guilty was what she deserved.

'I found another doctor. Somebody more sympathetic. I tried to talk with Moma about the drink and the drugs but she denied it and said I was making it up. After that she drank openly and it was a kind of nightmare. Finding drink and other things hidden away. The sight of Moma half out of her mind. I don't want to say any more about all that.' I was conscious of taking a deep breath. 'Then I came home one night and the place was empty. An hour later, a policewoman came to the door. Moma had been found dead in a shop doorway in Kensington.' I stopped for a minute to take another deep breath, and I heard Victoria say, 'Don't talk about it any more, Daddy. We understand. We really do.'

I looked at them both and said, 'I've told you all this because you'll hear it – totally distorted – some day. She didn't die of drink or drugs. She died because she'd been in the war. What had happened to Pauline and Violette was more than she could bear. If she hadn't been brave she would be alive today. She would never have volunteered for Special Operations Executive.'

For a moment they were silent and then Pauline said quietly, 'What happened to Violette?'

I was terribly tempted to make the point by telling her the truth. That Violette was the woman she'd described as "that old bag". But you don't do that to people you love. 'She's still around,' I said.

This story was first published by Woman and Home *in 1986 and was reprinted in the Dutch magazine* Margriet *that year.*

The members of the Special Forces Club in Herbert Crescent are men and women who served in one of the resistance forces such as SOE – Special Operations Executive. On the stairway up to the dining-room there are photographs of people who were exceptionally brave. I am always moved by seeing the photographs of young girls who are now elderly ladies or who long ago died in some concentration camp.

After the war the girls seemed to have more difficulty in settling down than the men and I wrote this story in remembrance of them.

Time Spent in Reconnaissance

Julie Peyton was twenty-two with dark hair, big brown eyes, a neat nose and a soft gentle mouth. She sat in the small cubicle with the earphones on, watching the dials on the tape recorder and looking up from time to time at the digital clock on the wall.

In the next room Peter Harvey was interrogating the Russian. Grinding away, asking the usual questions about meeting places, dates, names, who controlled him, where did he do his training? Then he'd go back over the same questions again. One of her duties was to note the discrepancies, the hesitations and evasions. Peter would probably notice them himself but she was there, or one of the other girls, as a back-up. When you couldn't see the person's face it gave an extra awareness of what was said.

It still seemed unbelievable to her. This rambling stately home not far from London. Set in its own grounds in the quiet country-side so that at night she could hear owls and, in the spring, the bleating of new-born lambs. Discreet guards patrolled the grounds and there were surveillance and security devices everywhere. Inside, the barred windows of the basement and the officers who could interrogate in almost every language in the world. And the steady flow of suspects and defectors laying out their tatty lives like offerings at a jumble sale. It all seemed a long way from college and the sixth form at Tunbridge Wells Grammar School for Girls.

Her father had always said that it was all very well to get a degree in some foreign language. But not Russian. How on earth would she earn a living from speaking Russian? Better get yourself a proper skill like shorthand and typing, he'd said. Mind you, he'd done the decent thing and paid for the crash course in what they called "secretarial skills". She had never told him what she did in her job.

She had still been on the secretarial course when she got the letter. It was from an address near Trafalgar Square. Would she like to come for an interview for a job in a government department where her Russian could be used?

There had been two men at the interview. One talking, one listening and watching. She was conscious of doing very badly. It was almost as if they didn't believe anything she said. There was nothing they said that was actually rude, but she disliked both of them long before the interview was halfway through. At the end of two hours, to her amazement, they offered her the job, to begin when she had finished her secretarial course.

There was no doubt that Peter Harvey was good-looking when he was relaxed. She liked him; admired his obvious talent but she had reservations. The hard lines of his mouth when he was interrogating, the half-closed eyes as he listened to the answers, disbelief so obvious on his face. But it was fair to say that that was what he was there for. Intelligence officers were trained to be like that. She remembered what they'd said on her course: 'Everybody tells lies about something. It pays to find out what it is.' And the course for the interrogators lasted for months, not the three weeks she had had. But give him his due, he was always amiable and friendly with her.

They had been going out together a couple of times a week for the last few months and he made it very clear that he liked her. She had taken him home once and she smiled to herself as she remembered her mother's comment: 'A nice-looking young man, very polite and all that. But I wouldn't want to meet him on a dark night.' For her mother, the whole male world was divided into those men whom she would or wouldn't like to meet on a dark night. But her mother had no idea what Peter's job was. She didn't even know what her daughter's job was. Secretary in a small government department was what they had suggested she said, and she'd stuck to it.

When Peter Harvey walked into the ops room he looked around for the girl. There was only Daphne Cooper.

'Where's Julie?'

'She's gone into town. She handed over to me about five minutes ago. She'll be back for your next session after lunch.'

'What bus did she catch?'

Daphne shrugged. 'I think she cadged a lift.'

'Who from?'

'I've no idea.'

Harvey walked down the corridor to the internal phone, picked it up and dialled two numbers.

'Is that transport . . .? Is Captain Palmer's car in the garage . . .? I see . . . when did he leave . . .? No, I just wanted to check if he was around . . . Thank you, Sergeant.'

He put back the receiver and his hand shook with suppressed anger. Palmer was a captain. In his late thirties. His immediate superior. A quiet man who adopted a fatherly approach to all the girls. They all liked Palmer. The reliable one, the shoulder to cry on. He and Palmer had had quite a good relationship until Julie came along. He was sure that Palmer had his eye on her. Probably impressing her with his superior rank. And making clear that Peter was just one of Palmer's juniors.

He finished the afternoon session at five and walked into her small annexe.

'What did you think of him?'

'Beginning to sound like a "plant".'

'Why?'

'He talked about meeting his contact at the Albert Theatre when he meant the Albert Hall. If he'd actually been there he'd have known its proper name. Said he was born and brought up in Moscow. But he's got a strong Georgian accent when he's tensed up.'

'Anything else?'

'He gave the same two dead-letter drops and at least one recognition sign that's been used before in phoney cover stories.'

He smiled. 'Did you get your shopping done at lunch-time?'

'Yes, thanks.'

'How did you manage to get there and back in an hour?'

'Hey, Peter. What is this – an interrogation? What I do in my lunch hour is nobody's business but mine.'

'I'm sorry. I'd better get moving.'

She looked up at his face and said softly, 'Don't get huffy, Peter. I like you and I admire the way you do your job, but I . . .'

He interrupted. 'I know what you mean. I apologise. How about I take you down to the coast on Sunday and we can relax and have a meal?'

She smiled. 'OK. Let's do that.'

*

21

At the weekly meeting Captain Palmer had gone over that week's interrogations with both of them.

'Any views on Malik, Peter?'

'There's a lot in his story that doesn't hang together. But what's really significant is that he has only told us things we know already. And it's all rather old hat, from last year rather than current stuff. Our experience of genuine defectors is that they're ready to come clean right up-to-date. All the questions I've put to him about his activities in the last few months have been evaded, or else he's given very vague answers.'

'What was your impression, Julie?'

For a moment she hesitated. It wasn't usual to ask the opinion of an assistant unless the interrogating officer initiated it himself. She knew that Peter Harvey would have noticed and been ruffled by it.

'I think Peter's right, sir.'

Palmer looked at Harvey. 'How much longer do you want to give him?'

'I think I'll leave him alone for a week or ten days, do some research on what he's said so far and then have another couple of days with him.'

'OK. Will you notify the duty scheduling officer tonight?'

Harvey made his point. 'I'll get Julie to do it after the meeting – sir.'

Captain Palmer had looked up sharply at the over-emphasised "sir". Palmer wasn't sure why it had been done. It was meant to be insolent but he classified it as juvenile. Showing off, for some unknown reason.

They sat on the beach after lunch. The sun was pleasantly warm and they sat watching the sailing boats tacking and weaving round the buoys in what was obviously some local regatta.

He was resting his chin in his hands, his elbows on his drawn-up knees and she said softly, 'What are you going to do when your six years are up?'

He shrugged. 'I don't really know. Maybe I'll sign on again provided I've had a promotion.'

'What did you do before?'

'Cambridge for the languages. And a year teaching.' He half-smiled. 'Not very successfully.'

'Do you like interrogating people?'

'Depends who they are. If they're trying it on, like friend

Malik, I like breaking them down. But some are pretty boring, as you know.' He paused and looked at her. 'What are you going to do?'

'Have four children. Two boys, two girls. A golden retriever and a thatched cottage in the country.'

He smiled. 'You're a romantic.'

'What's wrong with that?'

He shrugged. 'Nothing. I guess it's OK for girls.'

'Why not for men?'

'Men have to deal with reality. The real world.'

'And what *is* the real world?'

'It's where people lie and cheat. Where you have to look out for yourself. Make sure they don't put one over on you.'

'D'you really believe that?'

'Of course I do.'

She was silent for several minutes and then she said, 'Tell me about your parents. Where do they live?'

'My father is a bank manager. Lives in Leicester. Well, just outside.'

'And your mother?'

She probably wouldn't have noticed the moment's hesitation if it hadn't been for her training.

'She's just a housewife. Very beautiful. Very talented.'

'Talented at what?'

'She plays the piano. Could have been a concert pianist.'

It was an evening almost a week later, when they were the only staff playing tennis and they sat drinking a Coke in the small cedar-wood shelter facing the courts, that she asked him if he had had a girl-friend back home.

'Nobody special.'

'Did you go to dances and parties a lot?'

'No. I was always working.'

'Were you happy as a child?'

He frowned and said, 'Why are you asking all this?'

'I'd just like to know. You're my friend so I'd like to know about you.'

He half-smiled. 'I'm sorry I was sharp.' He paused. 'And I'm glad you said I'm your friend.'

'Were you an only child?'

'Yes.'

'Maybe that's why you're like you are.'

'Oh. And how am I?'

Julie sighed. 'You're a loner and sometimes I think you're lonely as well. If you'd had an unhappy love affair, that could have done it. If it isn't that then somebody must have done something to you.'

'Another amateur psychologist from the interrogation course, eh?'

She laughed softly. 'No. Not really. Anyway, I think you'll be a nice man when you're a bit older and you've learned to trust people.'

'Why is trusting people always considered a virtue?'

'Well, isn't it?' And she turned to look at his face.

'I don't see it as good or bad. Why get involved so that you have to decide one way or another? Just be independent . . . and then you won't be disappointed.'

'That means you'd never love someone.'

'How do you make that out?'

'Loving somebody means putting your head on the block and handing them the chopper, hoping they won't ever use it.'

He had gone into the dining-room as soon as the interrogation finished, hoping to see her there and take her to the cinema. He had booked one of the pool cars the day before, to make sure that he could take her out as his own car was being repaired. Mrs Fisher was the only one in the dining-room.

'Have you seen Julie at all, Mrs Fisher?'

'She asked me to tell you that she had to leave early. She had a telephone call. Her mother's poorly. She's gone to see her.'

He walked angrily to his office and phoned the transport section.

'I'm looking for Captain Palmer. Is his car there?'

'No, sir. He left about twenty minutes ago.'

'Was he able to contact Miss Peyton before he left, d'you know?'

'Yes. She was with him when he left.'

'Thanks.'

He slammed the phone down angrily. The lying little bitch. And that creep Palmer.

As Palmer drove through the outskirts of Bromley he asked her, 'How much further?'

'About five miles.'

'Don't worry, Julie. We'll soon be there.' He paused. 'How do you get on with the bright young man?'

'OK . . . I quite like him. But he seems a very closed up sort of fellow.'

'What's that mean?'

'He's terribly suspicious.'

'That's probably because of his job. We train interrogators to be suspicious.'

'He says everyone tells lies.'

'They do.' Palmer shrugged. 'They may be small lies, white lies, social lies. Making themselves more important than they really are.' He paused. 'What did he tell you about his parents?'

'He said his father was a bank manager.'

'And his mother?'

'Just that she was very beautiful and a very talented pianist.'

Palmer sighed. 'Take a tip from me. Never talk about his mother.'

'Why not? He's obviously very fond of her.'

'Momma Harvey walked out on her husband and son when the boy was eight years old. She wasn't beautiful but she was pretty. She was a stripper before she married and she went off with the manager of a club. He threw her out two years later. She was passed around the third-rate clubs for three more years and finally she ended up in a unit for alcoholics in St Albans. Literally ended up. She died there.'

'God, how terrible. Does he know all this?'

'Oh, yes. He knows.'

'No wonder he made up that story.'

'You mean, no wonder he lied.'

'If it's a lie, it's a forgivable one.'

'He could have just said that she was dead.'

'You're awfully hard on him.'

Palmer smiled. 'I'm not. I was just testing your reactions. Character probing.'

'And what did you find?'

'A generous mind. A sympathetic heart. You'll do.'

At breakfast the next morning Palmer took his coffee over to the table where Harvey was sitting alone. As he sat down he said, 'You look as though you didn't get much sleep last night, Peter.'

'I didn't.' He glanced at Palmer as he said, 'And how was your evening out?'

'It wasn't improved by your telegram.'

'She showed it to you, did she?'

'No. But I read it.'

'That was a bit off, wasn't it? Reading other people's private mail?'

'Was it really necessary? The people at her Post Office will have read it.' He looked directly at Harvey's face. 'What were those elegant words? "Dear Julie – You're a lying bitch. I've had enough, Peter Harvey."' He paused. 'Charming.'

'She *is* a lying bitch and you know it. She swanned off with you instead of me. She had a date with me. Left a message saying her mother was ill, or something.'

For a moment Palmer was silent and then he said quietly, 'Maybe it's time you had a change of job, Peter. Your work seems to be getting mixed up with your private life.'

'What's that mean?' The younger man's aggression was all too obvious as he spoke.

'You have to spend your working hours suspecting people. Looking for their lies. Digging holes for them to drop into. You're beginning to do the same in your private life.'

'You mean I should be the normal male sucker with girls?'

Palmer shook his head. 'No. I mean that the people you interrogate are already suspect. Your friends aren't suspects . . . or shouldn't be.'

Harvey's voice was shrill with suppressed anger and indignation. 'For Christ's sake. She broke a date with me to go swanning off with you. If you don't really believe me, ask her.'

'I can't, unfortunately. She's not here.' Palmer looked at Harvey's face. 'I wouldn't ask her, anyway.'

'Where is she? She's got no leave due.'

'You could end up quite a bright fellow, Harvey. But you've got a lot to learn. Learn the lesson that's staring you in the face right now.'

'And what lesson is that?'

'That if you want to find out if somebody's telling you lies you actually have to find out. Not just assume that they're lying because it suits you to think so.'

'I don't get it.'

Palmer looked across the room and then back at the young man as he said quietly, 'Her mother was already dead when we got there. Julie's staying on for the funeral.'

The shock on Peter Harvey's face was instant and obvious. 'Oh my God,' he whispered. 'How terrible.'

Palmer waited until the news had sunk in and then said, 'Why don't you go up and see her? She's much in need of a shoulder to cry on.'

'God, I couldn't face her. Not after that bloody telegram.'

Palmer reached inside his jacket and took out a folded piece of paper. 'Here. Take it. There's your telegram. She never saw it. I took it from the boy and opened it in case it was something that needed dealing with. I saw what it said and I saw it was from you. I thought it might be better to keep it.' He paused. 'You can take a forty-eight-hour pass and a warrant. Get it from the clerk and I'll sign it.' He added softly, 'And if it helps you, I never was a rival. I'm married. Happily married. Julie knew that. She'd had a look in my "P" file. And she met my wife the other day when I took her to town. Always remember that old army precept, Peter: "Time spent in reconnaissance is seldom wasted."'

This story was first published in Woman's Own *in 1984.*

THE RED MUSTANG

Almost six feet of the wall was covered with cork board, and there were about twenty photographs pinned to the board. They were photographs of men's faces, some crisp and clear, some very grainy because they had been taken furtively in bad light. Across the top of the board was a hand-drawn notice on white card that said, in Russian, "Know your Enemy". And under each photograph was a typed slip that gave brief details of the man in the picture. His name, his rank and where he worked, and a file reference number. They were CIA officers. Three in Moscow, two in Warsaw, two in Paris, four in West Germany in Bonn, Hamburg and West Berlin. They were mostly young faces, some of them good-looking, but the older men had faces that looked worn and their eyes looked resentful and shaded with disbelief. Some of the details were out of date and at least one was dead. And right in the middle of the photographs some joker had tacked up a page from an American magazine. It was in full colour and showed a red convertible Mustang driven by a smiling man, his companion a beautiful blonde whose long hair streamed out in the breeze.

It was after midnight,. and Viktor Petrov sat looking at the pictures without seeing them because he was trying to decide once and for all what he should do. The old-fashioned office was a temporary work-place for KGB officers of the First Office of the First Directorate in KGB headquarters in Dzerdzhinski Square. The department that was responsible for operations against the Americans. Not that Petrov was working against the Americans, he worked in West Germany. The reason why he was there so late was that he was trying finally to decide whether to defect to the Americans or stay put. He had made his mind up to do it a dozen times in the last six months but he needed some salve to his conscience and now he had the best possible reason. He had been passed over for promotion and that fool Tartakov was going to be his new boss. They had been bitter rivals since their early days together at the Frunze training school.

But that wasn't the real reason he wanted to defect. The real reason was that he was bored. Bored with his wife and tired of having the responsibilities of a husband and a father. He had found the whole set-up irksome for nearly two years. He wanted to be like the man in the red Mustang with the pretty blonde. Footloose and fancy-free. He didn't blame Natasha and certainly not his son. He was thirty-nine and she was ten years younger. Still pretty and attractive, but boring. And she no longer aroused his desire. It had been wild and exciting in those early years but for the last nine years she had been more mother than wife. There were things you couldn't do to a wife and more things that you couldn't do to a mother. Even he had to admit to himself that she was a good wife and an excellent mother. But now that he'd been passed over for Tartakov that was the last straw. It almost wasn't his decision. They, the idiots here in Moscow, had made the decision for him.

He was due back in Bonn in ten days' time and he would plan it out in the meantime. When he stood up he leaned forward and tore the picture of the Mustang from its pin, folded it in four and slid it into his inside pocket. Nobody would miss it. The room was only used by transient officers awaiting a firm posting.

The day before he was due to return to Bonn they had gone on a boat trip on the Moskva, then in the afternoon they had taken Yuri to the circus.

In the evening he had taken Natasha to the Bolshoi and afterwards they had eaten at the National on Marx Prospekt. They had walked back to their apartment and, despite the pleasant family day, he was glad that he felt no guilt about what he was going to do.

She was tired and went straight to bed and, when he had packed his bags, he stood looking at her face on the pillow where it was lit by the pink-shaded bedside lamp.

He was going to send them a letter when he was safely in the USA and make it clear that she knew nothing of his plan to defect.

She'd lose all the privileges that KGB wives got but she'd never set much store by them, anyway. He had told her not to go with him in the morning to see him off at Sheremetyevo. It would look better for her that way.

He switched off the bedside lamp and checked that his digital watch alarm was set for 6 a.m.

The Aeroflot flight to Bonn was uneventful and he went to the room he rented in Bad Godesburg. He had four days to get through before he actually did it and when he went to the office, Tartakov's attitude only confirmed his decision. It would round things off neatly if Tartakov lost his promotion because one of his senior staff had defected in the first month after he took over.

There were routine jobs that he had to do but he spent as much time as he dared gathering up information that would interest the Americans. His own work was solely concerned with West German affairs but there were others who covered the Americans – their diplomats, their military establishments and the US Embassy staff, especially the German nationals.

He stood on the other side of the street looking at all the lights in the US Embassy building. It was the Thanksgiving Day celebration for the Americans in Bonn and their guests. He could hear the faint sounds of music and big limousines were still being waved into the temporary car-park by uniformed marines. Diplomats from society dinners and ministers from late meetings in ornate offices. He walked across the road, then through the open gates and along the gravel drive to the brightly lit portico of the embassy. A US marine sergeant stopped him as he got to the open door, smiling amiably as he said, 'May I see your invitation, sir?'

'I want to see an intelligence officer.'

'I suggest you call tomorrow, sir. All the embassy staff are off-duty tonight.'

'I can't wait till tomorrow, I need to see someone now.' He paused and said quietly, 'I'm a KGB officer.'

'Can I ask what it's about?'

'Yes, I want to ask for political asylum.'

For a moment the sergeant hesitated, then he said, 'You'd better come with me.'

They walked down a wide corridor where groups of people were talking and laughing as they helped themselves to drinks from the small tables. Then the music was loud as they reached tall double doors.

'Just wait here, sir. I'll be right back.'

There was a band playing up on a dais and a girl singer stood at the microphone. She was singing "The Yellow Rose of Texas". The room was so crowded that there was hardly room for the couples to dance, and they were hindered by groups of people standing talking.

He saw the sergeant make his way to one of those groups and speak to a tall man in the dress uniform of the US Navy. He had to lean forward to hear what the sergeant was saying, then he looked towards the door, his eyes searching. The officer said something to the pretty girl beside him and then threaded his way through the crowd to the door, accompanied by the sergeant. The officer nodded to him to follow them down a side corridor. Nobody spoke until they were in a small room with just a table and some plain wooden chairs.

Then the officer turned to look at him.

'I'm told you want to talk to somebody. Can I help you?'

'My name's Viktor Petrov and I'm a major in the KGB. I ask for political asylum.'

'Have you got any identification?'

Petrov reached for his inside jacket pocket and took out his passport and his KGB identity card and handed them over. The officer checked the pages slowly and checked his face against both photographs before handing them back.

'Make yourself comfortable. The sergeant will take care of you.'

No Intelligence service likes "walk-ins". Not the CIA, nor MI6, nor the KGB. They like defections to be planned. The defector can be expected to provide agreed information before coming over. It gives time to test his strength of purpose and check his background if it isn't already known. But a defector who just walks in may be a "plant" by the other side, and he has no value beyond filling gaps in what is already known. "Walk-ins" can only provide history, and Intelligence services want the future – support or contradiction of their constant crystal-ball gazing. It is vital to establish the motives of a "walk-in" defector. Why has he come over, and why now?

On the top floor of the embassy was a long narrow room; one of the long walls was crammed with TV monitors, laser printers, a panel of high-powered transceivers and an array of full-sized tape-recorders. Two men stood watching the screen of a separate control panel on a table as a printer chattered away beside it. The message from Washington was brief.

State and Langley agree acceptance at your discretion. Deliver Stateside soonest ex-Frankfurt. Subject PETROV VIKTOR ANDREIVICH. Age 39. Married, one child, son. Known KGB. Thought to be 1st Dep of Ist Dir. Last rank registered, captain. Operates FRG out of Bonn. Cover journalist for Novosty. File SU/94/1748/93 Stop.

It was over an hour since Petrov had walked into the embassy and he had already been taken to a house on the outskirts of Bonn.

Petrov saw the two men come into the room. The older man nodded to the marine guard, who snapped to attention before leaving the room. The older man introduced himself.

'Major Petrov, my name's McQueen, and my colleague here is Pete Hodiak.' He paused. 'Have they been looking after you OK?'

Petrov nodded. 'Yes, thank you.'

'By the way, we have you on our records as a captain. When were you promoted?'

'Nearly a year ago.'

McQueen laughed and shrugged. 'I guess somebody's slipping.' He paused. 'Pete's going to stay here with you tonight. Tomorrow we'll be taking you down to Frankfurt and then on to the States.' McQueen looked at Petrov and then said quietly, 'If you change your mind overnight, just tell Pete in the morning and the book's closed. We won't talk. OK?'

'Thanks.'

McQueen nodded to Pete Hodiak. 'See you tomorrow, Pete. The car will be here at eight.'

McQueen didn't actually leave the house and it was two hours later when Hodiak went up to his room. A marine in civilian clothes was guarding the Russian's room.

Hodiak settled himself in one of the two comfortable armchairs and turned to McQueen.

'What did you think? First impressions.'

'Looked bright but scared, but that's par for the course.' He smiled. 'Now tell me your bit.'

33

'Well, he's not going to change his mind, that's for sure.'

'Why does he want to come over?'

Hodiak smiled. 'The usual reasons. A bit of everything. I'd guess he's got problems at home and in his work. I think he fancies the good life. If he was one of ours, I'd say he's a swinger.' He grinned. 'A yuppy from Moscow.'

'What's he got to trade?'

'I didn't probe but I'd guess it's enough, but it's going to take time. He needs to sort himself out.'

'Sounds like something for you, and he's more your age. I'll do the straight stuff and you can act like his best buddy.' McQueen shrugged. 'I need some sleep.'

The next day they flew direct to Washington where a car took them out to CIA headquarters at Langley. Petrov was put through the standard processing. Personal details, fingerprints, photographs and a medical check. He was taken for a polygraph test which, as usual, proved inconclusive. They slept in one of the night duty-officers' rooms and the next day the three of them flew down to Los Angeles where a car and driver were waiting for them.

They were driven down to San Diego, to a clapboard house overlooking the beach off La Jolla Boulevard.

As they sat on the verandah with drinks, McQueen said, 'Where'd you learn your good English, Viktor?'

'At school, at Moscow University and I did two years in London.'

'And you speak good German, too?'

Petrov smiled and shrugged. 'It's not bad.'

Hodiak poured another drink for each of them and then looked at Petrov. 'I'll take you into La Jolla tomorrow and we'll get you some more suitable clothes. Something a bit more casual.'

They went on talking and Hodiak was aware that Petrov was frequently turning to look at the people on the beach. And finally Hodiak said, 'We'll go for a swim tomorrow.'

'Are the girls in films?'

Hodiak laughed. 'No, they'll just be secretaries and local girls.'

'They're all so beautiful. Like film stars.'

'It's the sun and the good life, Viktor. You'll meet some of them when we go for a swim.'

When Hodiak was driving Petrov back from the shopping trip to La Jolla, Petrov said, 'I suppose you want to start interrogating me?'

Hodiak smiled. 'We call it de-briefing. Sounds friendlier.'

The Russian shrugged. 'We're both professionals. We both know the rules of the game.'

'What *are* the rules, so far as you're concerned?'

'I accept that when a guy defects, there's a price to pay. Information. Names, responsibilities, background. Who matters, who doesn't. Who's doing what, and where.'

'There's no hurry. Get yourself settled and then we'll talk.'

They went down to the beach in the afternoon. Hodiak introduced him to several acquaintances including a couple of pretty girls and Petrov was obviously taken with one of the girls. He took Hodiak to one side and asked if he was allowed to ask her for a date. Hodiak suggested that he dated the girl the following week, to give them time to construct his new identity. The American was aware that Petrov was as eager for the date as some college boy, despite the fact that he was nearly forty years old. But it was not uncommon for Soviet defectors to want to make up for the lost time of a life that had been totally controlled by an ever-watchful regime. Anything that helped him settle in was all to the good.

After three months they had got most of what they wanted from Petrov. He had been given a new identity, a social security number, an IRS tax clearance certificate and a retainer that allowed him to live reasonably well. With an offer of additional payments if he wanted to act as a consultant for CIA operations in Germany. With his new name of Victor Peters he had been given a two-year-free rental of a similar but smaller house a mile up the coast. Arrangements had been made with a CIA-controlled company for Victor Peters to act as their local insurance broker. And he now had a pretty girl-friend named Joanna who was twenty years old.

Moscow assumed at first that Petrov had defected to the West Germans, but when their protests had been angrily rejected by Bonn they turned their attention to Washington. After the usual ritual denials, Washington had eventually agreed that Petrov had been granted political asylum. The Soviet Embassy demanded the opportunity of interviewing Petrov. Both he and the State Department refused. A letter which the Soviet Embassy's First Secretary said was from Petrov's wife was handed over and passed to Petrov. He put it in his desk drawer at home without opening it. It was a reminder of a past he wanted to forget.

He was on his own now, with Joanna as his steady girl-friend.

Pete Hodiak visited him once a week without invitation. Sometimes in his small office in La Jolla and sometimes at his house. They got on well together and Petrov suspected that a lot of his insurance business came through the CIA man, who was stationed permanently now in the CIA's office in Los Angeles.

The first time that he had a quarrel with Joanna, his anger had quickly turned into depression. In the middle of a sleepless night he had gone to his desk and taken out Natasha's letter. He knew it was genuine because it was her neat handwriting that had written his name on the envelope. He found himself still walking around with the unopened letter in his hand when the dawn came. Holding it as if it were a bomb that would explode any minute. Tempted to tear it open. Desperate for even a remote contact with someone who really knew him. Not short-term friends like Joanna and Pete Hodiak. It was lying on the floor beside his bed when the phone woke him a few hours later.

It was Joanna, who didn't seem to be aware that they had quarrelled as she told him that her boss had given her two tickets to a private showing at an art gallery on Juan Street in San Diego that evening. And suddenly his depression had gone. It was an OK world again.

Just as a standard routine Hodiak arranged for Petrov's home to be checked, while he was at his office, by a high-tech CIA search team. They reported the unopened letter in Petrov's desk and they also reported that Petrov's radio was tuned to the frequency of Moscow's North American service in English. They had used a device to read the letter without opening it. It was decided that the house should be wired, the telephone tapped, and that future checks would be weekly.

Hodiak was asleep when the phone rang and he checked his watch before reaching for the phone. It was 4.15 a.m. McQueen was calling from Washington.

'I've just had a call, Pete, from our monitoring unit at White Plains overseas exchange. I understand your people have been monitoring in and out telephone calls from our mutual friend in La Jolla.'

'Yeah.'

'You'd better get over there and listen to the tape for last Tuesday at two a.m. I'll fly down tomorrow and we'll talk.'

Hodiak was in the LA office two hours later. He read the typed transcript and listened three times to the tape. Then he read the transcript again. The bit that mattered was quite brief.

All copy in Russian. Time of call: 0205

Operator (female): 'Moscow exchange – what number?'
Petrov: '2336356'

Calling tone 19 seconds. Phone picked up.

Respondent (female): 'Who is it?'
Petrov: 'It's me, Tasha.'
Respondent: 'Is that really you, Victor?'
Petrov: 'Yes. How are you?'
Respondent: 'Things are very bad here.'
Petrov: 'Tell me.'
Respondent: 'They confiscated our bank account. Yuri has been expelled from his school. He's very upset. Nobody talks to me any more. Just my mother.'
Petrov: 'What do you live on?'
Respondent: 'I've been allocated a job in an engineering factory. It pays only seventy-five roubles a month. I'm just selling everything bit by bit. They said we're all guilty under the law and . . . (Respondent distressed) . . . oh, Victor, what shall . . .?'

Line cut at this point.

Hodiak checked with Langley on McQueen's flight and met him at LAX. They went to the coffee bar to talk. When the coffee had been served McQueen said, 'What did you think?'
'The KGB are playing games.'
'Why do you think that?'
'He phoned his old house number and she was there. They wouldn't have left her in a privileged apartment for any other reason than the chance that he might call her.'
'You're right. Does he talk about her at all?'
'When he's down he does. He seems to think his girl-friend Joanna is like his wife was when he first knew her. I don't think she is, from what he's told me. But he seems to think so.'
'So what do we do?'

'Let me get back alongside him again and see what's going on.'

'I'll hang around for a couple of days, so keep me in touch.'

Hodiak was sitting on the porch steps of Petrov's house when he got back from work.

'Hi, Victor. How're you making out?'

Petrov shrugged. 'I'm OK.'

'You sound a bit down. D'you want a drink?'

'There are drinks inside.'

'You got a beer?'

'Yeah. Come on in.'

As they sat in the comfortable armchairs with their beers Hodiak said, 'How's business?'

'Very good.'

'And Joanna?'

'She's OK.'

'And you? How're you?'

For a moment Petrov hesitated and then he said, 'I don't belong here, Pete.'

'I thought you liked it – the sunshine, the beach, Joanna. You've got a great life. What's wrong?'

'I've got no roots here.' He shrugged. 'I've got no roots anywhere, any more. It's a kind of . . . a kind of limbo. Like an old man waiting to die.'

'Has something happened to make you feel this way?'

'No. It's just me. I don't know what I'm doing here. I don't know where I'm at. I wish now I'd never come over.'

'Do you want to go back?'

'Good God, no. I'd be in one of the Gulag camps in the time it takes the waggons to get there.'

'So what did you do wrong that's worrying you?'

'Nothing really. I guess I was just a sucker for the American dream.'

'And you haven't found it lives up to your expectations?'

'No. It's not that.' He sighed. It's like being in a play by Tolstoy but you keep mouthing the lines for a Chekhov play. Nothing wrong with the words. Just that they don't fit.'

'Anything I can do to help?'

Petrov shook his head. 'Thanks, but no. It's just a question of time. Something good will happen and I'll be OK again.'

*

McQueen was an old LA hand and always stayed at the Tiverton Terrace in Westwood, and that's where Hodiak met him the same night. They sat in McQueen's pleasant bedroom with a bottle of bourbon between them.

'Tell me,' McQueen said.

'I've been thinking about it on the way up. I think the mistake we made with Petrov is not recognising that, despite being KGB, he's really rather naive. He didn't know much about the USA – just films and magazines. Just imagine you or me in Moscow. All we've ever heard about Russia is from sitreps and books and news-clips on TV. But we don't know a damn thing about how ordinary people live. How to get the plumbing fixed, or a haircut, or a guy to fix the car. It's all there and everybody else knows where it is. But not us. And it'll take us a long time to find out.'

McQueen smiled. 'Sounds like Washington.'

Hodiak didn't respond. 'We suck him dry and then give him what he wants – freedom. George – you need training before you can cope with freedom. That poor bastard is a lost soul. Lonely – so he phones his wife. That gives him a guilt complex a mile wide. It's sunny and he makes enough bread, but where's Fred Astaire and Ginger Rogers? It's just Moscow with sun and money.'

'So what do we do?'

'We accept that he's just a grown-up kid. He needs a prize every now and again. So we give him one.'

'What, for instance?'

'Remember when he walked in that night in Bonn? We checked him over and found that ad from *Life* magazine. The red Mustang and the blonde.'

'So?'

'I can get a deal on a used Mustang convertible for under five hundred bucks.'

'Like giving a kid a lollipop.'

'Yeah, I guess so.'

'You think it'll stop him from doing a bunk?'

'I don't think that's even in his mind. If that's what he had in mind he wouldn't be so confused.'

'OK. Take it from the contingency fund and put in a chit.' He looked at Hodiak. 'I hope it's as simple as you think.'

When Hodiak drove up to Petrov's place that evening with the red convertible Mustang, the look on the Russian's face when he told him it was his made him sure that it was just the right move. There were plenty of Americans older than Petrov who still secretly fancied a red Mustang. And there was always a blonde in the passenger seat. It wasn't the money that stopped them. It was less than five hundred bucks. What put people off was the very image that attracted them. It was an image from way back. An image that was too self-revealing. Like having *Penthouse* delivered at home instead of picking it up from a sidewalk news stand. But there was no doubt that it worked its magic on the Russian.

Pete Hodiak and his wife had booked in for three nights at the Beverly Hills Comstock over New Year and they were actually packing to go home when the phone rang.

'Hodiak.'

'Pete, it's Joanna . . . why did he do it?' She was obviously very distressed.

'Who's done what, honey?'

'Victor.'

'What did he do?'

'He's dead. He killed himself.'

'When was this?'

'Last night. We'd been to a party and he seemed fine. We came back to my place and watched TV, and he walked out. I thought he'd gone to the bathroom. When he didn't come back I went down to the street to his car, but it was gone. I was annoyed because I thought he'd stood me up and I rang his number to tell him so, but there was no answer. About an hour ago the police came here. He'd gone to the coast somewhere near Torrey Pines and driven the car off the end of the jetty into the sea. The hood was down and his seat-belt was fastened. They said it was obviously deliberate.'

'Had he been drinking a lot?'

'No. A couple of vodkas and a glass of wine. He sure wasn't drunk.'

'You hadn't had a row or anything?'

'No. We just watched the movie on TV.'

'What was the movie?'

'It was the old *Dr Zhivago* film.'

'We'll be down there in about three hours. We'll pick you up.'

'Why did he do it, Pete? He was a nice guy.'

'I don't know, honey.' He hung up, and he did know.

I think that Philby, Maclean and Burgess were the last people to defect to the Soviet Union for ideological reasons. They were believers rather than self-servers. Perestroika and glasnost have revealed how mistaken they were. Once they were in Moscow they must have realised how different the reality was from the dream. These days defectors come over to the West for more practical reasons – mainly the "good life" and things like beautiful blondes and red Mustangs.

Back in 1966 I had a bright red Mustang myself and I loved it. It was one of the first in this country and it cost me a packet in upkeep because small boys used to steal the hub-caps which were very fancy and very expensive. And my lady is brunette and even more beautiful.

THE GIRL FROM ADDIS

On April the 5th 1941 we liberated Addis Ababa. Wingate from the north and Platt from the south. MI6 had sent me in with Wingate's lot, and my official title and cover was Military Liaison Officer to the Emperor, His Royal Highness Haile Selassie, King of Kings, the Lion of Judah. He was a small neat little man with big brown eyes.

We spoke only in French. He said it was because it was the language of diplomacy, but I always reckoned it was his way of telling us that he wasn't going to do any bowing and scraping to the British just because we'd liberated his country. But he was always quite nice to me until they rumbled what I was really up to.

A couple of days after the liberation there had been the big ceremony in front of the Palace; mainly to give Wingate a chance to ride in on a white horse. He was a fine figure of a man but even his most ardent admirers admitted that he was a bit eccentric. The rest of us thought he was just plain nuts.

The high point of the ceremonies was to be a dispatch rider of the Royal Corps of Signals riding in on his BSA 500 with the first mail to the liberated country. The top letter was to be from King George VI saying welcome back to the club to his fellow Highness. As Military Liaison Officer I was to take the bundle of mail, open the top letter, pass it to the Emperor and he would read it with the aid of the loudspeakers to the assembled mob. And surprise, surprise, it would be from the friendly King in London.

Some guardian angel made me glance at the open letter as I passed it to His Nibs and I saw to my horror the letter-head of a well-known furniture removers. It was from their office in Bath. It was brief and to the point. The sum of £471 was eight months overdue for storage of the royal furniture and unless payment was made in seven days, etc, etc. His big soft brown eyes looked up from the letter to my face. He turned to the microphone and spoke in Amharic. And against the roar of applause he told me that I would be reading the King's message.

I don't know what the King actually wrote because we never found his letter, but, with visions of the Tower of London and courts martial, I made it up as I went along. The second verse of "Land of Hope and Glory" came into it somewhere, and despite what the embassy people said later, it was received rapturously by the assembled thousands.

The Emperor never mentioned the incident again. Neither did I. But years later I saw our dear Ambassador's report to the Foreign Office. "Jingoist" and "fit for a *Daily Express* editorial" are the bits that stick in my mind.

Apart from the PWs in camps there were quite a lot of Italians in Addis. The Palace wasn't keen to let them go. They knew how to repair cars and radios, and build buildings, and administer the law. The Italians saw through me right from the start. They were used to reading the signs and portents, and a British Officer who was shunned by the Embassy, openly snubbed by the British Military Mission, and who bought his petrol on the black-market, stuck out like a sore thumb. There wasn't much that went on that I didn't get to hear about, as they were under the impression that a word from me could land them back in a PW camp, and I did nothing to disabuse them.

It took the Ethiopians nearly a year to work out what I was up to, and the first I knew that my cover was blown was after a reception for the Greek Ambassador at the Old Palace.

The Colonel of the Imperial Guard had escorted me across the parade ground and suggested we had a look at the new stables. Mamu was in the first one. He was from Harar, about fifteen years old. He lay on some filthy straw and Colonel Mulugueta had pointed at Mamu's feet with his stick. The bones that stuck through the flesh were a beautiful dazzling white, and despite his dark skin the raw, red meat where they'd smashed at him was an even darker red. There was not much blood but that was because he'd been dead for some time. Mamu was my house-boy.

Mulugueta's smoky eyes had watched carefully as I read the note he handed to me. It was signed by His Imperial Highness and was in French. I was persona non grata and I'd got forty-eight hours to get out.

I walked across to the Imperial Hotel and phoned the embassy. They didn't want to know. But they condescended to send a signal for me to London and Nairobi.

I lived in a block at the bottom of the hill, alongside the tin shanties, and I went back there to wait. I wasn't going just on the Emperor's say so. If they put me inside I'd at least have the pleasure of knowing that HM Ambassador would have to swallow his prejudices and try and negotiate me out. And if that failed the Military Mission would have to give up their polo for half a day and brush up on "Platoon in Attack".

The flat was one room and a kitchen and bathroom. White-painted walls and a single divan against the wall. When Maria came to stay at weekends or for odd nights I'd get flowers from the market, but otherwise it was a rather monastic pad. The filing cabinets took up more space than anything else.

There was only one thing in Addis that London really cared about at that time and that was the Kanassian business. Kanassian was a merchant with bases all over that neck of the woods: Asmara, Addis, Dire-Dawa, Aden and the Yemen. He was an Armenian, a widower with two small children and a millionaire several times over. He had influence everywhere: with the Italians, the Vichy French, the Arabs, the Emperor, and the British at all the top levels.

Like the locals I had to buy my petrol and car spares on the black-market. And that meant that I was buying from Kanassian. I had been in Addis for about a month when a small truck delivered four brand new tyres for my car. I hadn't ordered them. Tyres were one hundred pounds each. They were a gift from Kanassian. I sent them back with a friendly note. I had had one of his dhows from Aden intercepted by the Royal Navy who had confiscated the cargo and sent it on its way. The cargo was rifles and .303 ammunition on its way to Berbera.

Although Kanassian was frequently invited to our embassy parties, I was not. But our paths crossed at the receptions at the Palace and at parties at the Greek and Swedish Embassies. He was never embarrassed, always amiable, and he would stroll over to chat with me as if we were old friends. He was a stockily built man, broad shouldered and heavy featured. His thick black hair was a mass of tight curls and his eyes were a yellowy-green like the eyes of a bird of prey. He would stand there, his drink in one hand, the other resting on my arm, and we would talk about Matisse and Seurat or Delibes and Debussy. Never about guns or drugs. He wasn't a bluffer, his interest in art and music was genuine enough. But every now and again there would be a subtle question about my background, my finances, my taste in girls and my prospects when the war was over.

From time to time he invited me to his village and he accepted my excuses with good grace. He had come personally to my apartment one evening to deliver half a dozen Charles Trenet records. Fortunately I had been out and they had been handed over to Mamu. In fact I'd been watching as he got into his car outside his offices, not knowing that he was driving to my place. I'd decided to take a risk and have a look in his offices. There had been nothing except a thick code book. The pages were typed, not printed, and I'd torn out one of the back pages. He had transceivers at both Addis and Aden but they were permanently monitored by Signals Security who had not found anything to excite me. Some illegal transferring of sterling but nothing more.

The page had gone back to London in the diplomatic bag and I assumed that I should hear no more. Ten days later I got a brown envelope from the embassy that was heavy with red sealing-wax and pink tape.

Bletchley had taken one look at the page of code and identified it as the current Japanese naval code, and London were sweating on the top line. It seemed that Japanese submarines had been sinking our merchant ships in the Indian Ocean at what should have been impossible distances. The only explanation was that there must be mother-ships refuelling the subs that the Royal Navy had not accounted for. There were two identified supply ships but naval intelligence swore that they couldn't supply so many subs with naphtha so far from their Tokyo base. There was no Axis or neutral port that could be supplying the mother-ships. My lot had suggested that it might be Kanassian. But the Navy at Aden couldn't believe that their old friend was playing footsie with the Japs. After all it was only thanks to the Royal Navy and the Merchant Navy that he got naphtha and petrol at all.

Then Signals Security sent a detector van down to Dire-Dawa and sat outside the town for a couple of weeks. They intercepted a signal in the Jap Navy code and estimated its source.

The RAF took me over the suspect area and a couple of miles south of the estimate I saw what I was looking for. A small island, marked on the charts as Socotra Island. I went out on a destroyer and the 40-gallon drums were neatly laid out under the camouflaged rubber sheets. There were over 4,000 gallons and it took a day and a night to get them on board.

There was nothing to link them with Kanassian except suspicion. London's suspicion and mine. MI6 said that I was to drop everything except the pursuit of Kanassian.

It had been after I found gold yen in the market of Addis that London had really hardened up. I had traced the gold yen back to Kanassian's place in Addis. And there was nobody else in the area who had sufficient fuel to interest the Japanese Navy. But the warning from London had been clear – "Don't pull him in until you've got the kind of evidence that would stand up in court". Kanassian's influence was at top level, and I was getting the red light. If I put him inside while short of evidence, then a lot of heads would roll. And mine would be at the very bottom of the pile.

The Third Secretary brought round Nairobi's reply a couple of hours later. My replacement would be flown over from Aden that night and I was to hand over to him at Kathi Kathiki's night-club. At midnight I was to destroy all the files and hand over verbally. I was to keep on the move.

It took two hours burning all the papers on the kitchen stove and pounding the ashes to dust, but when I'd finished I put on the battered portable gramophone and listened for the last time to Josephine Baker's thin, fluting voice singing *"J'ai deux amours, mon pays et Paris"*. I drank another coffee, lit a cigarette and sat there thinking. It must have been Kanassian or one of his people who had tipped them off. I'd been fairly careful and they wouldn't have added it up themselves. But why hadn't he done it before? Maybe I was getting too near. Whatever it was, he was showing the world that he could play games against the British Intelligence service, and win.

I left the door of the flat wide open, picked up my bags and went down to the car. It was a Lancia Aprillia, an elegant black one, a lovely car provided you didn't mind the gear lever coming adrift in your hand from time to time.

I parked my bags at the Imperial and took a bath. The word had not gone around yet and everybody was very polite.

They'd called the city Addis Ababa – the New Flower; and despite its squalor, they were right. There's no other city in the world like Addis. There was a vital spark in the people, hard to describe because it was not connected with energy, not even with progress. It was something to do with eternal things, biblical things.

47

Somebody once said that we all know what went on at Sodom, but what went on at Gomorrah? The people of Addis would know. There was no vice, no lust, that couldn't be slaked in Addis. And the blue gums, the bougainvillaea and the jacaranda trees were a lush and fitting setting. Maybe it was nothing more than the effect of living eight thousand feet above sea level.

There were a few goodbyes to say, where security would have to take its chance, and I walked down the long street to the Magalla.

Down the side streets the evening sun could get no foothold, and in the bars the Addis harlots were already assembling. They clustered and twittered like exotic birds, pretty, alive, and with figures that promised the poet's delight of "pneumatic bliss". To call them prostitutes would be too harsh; they were too young, too beautiful, too innocently available; they were biblical harlots straight out of the Old Testament. Their bodies were as sleek as an otter's and they could be yours all night for a pound, all week for a monkey skin handbag.

The market was still busy, and there were stalls selling "*tej*" and "*wot*", checked cloth, coffee and tobacco. In some of the wall-shops there was filigree silver and yellow Abyssinian gold in bracelets, bangles and long delicate chains. There were all the usual heaps of cereals and pulses, and corded piles of skins and hides. Goats were tethered in groups with game birds strung up on poles, alive, with their beady eyes blinking as they hung upside down with their wings half-open.

I turned into the second narrow street down the hill and walked into Biffi's restaurant. It was called "The Star of Ethiopia" and the sign outside was in English, French and Amharic. Emilio Biffi had been a sergeant in the Italian army and after being taken prisoner at Adowa he had been transported to Addis.

Biffi was one of those who had stayed behind. He hadn't had any choice but he didn't complain. And with a prosperous bar and ten pretty girls on the premises, he had no reason to.

As I pushed aside the long bead curtain on the door, Biffi poked his head out of the back room and saw me. He smiled, waved and walked over. He called to one of the girls.

'Two whiskies. From *my* bottle.'

He pointed to a chair and we sat waiting for the drinks at the table. There were a dozen or so girls swaying and clicking their fingers to the music. Biffi gave me a vivid description of their hidden attributes and their current state of health. His brown eyes looked at me with sympathy.

'I hear they kill your boy, yes?'

'Yes. When did you hear it?'

'This morning. They tell plenty people.'

'What else did they tell them?'

'They say you are spy against the Emperor and you got to leave, *subito*.'

'I'm leaving late tonight.'

'How you get back, *Capitano*?'

'They're sending a plane from Aden.'

'You want I tell her that you are here?'

'Is she here?'

He stood up. 'I tell her you want see her.'

Five minutes later she came in. I can still say that she was the most beautiful girl I've ever seen. Her skin was the colour of a copper beech in winter and smooth as a stone from an Atlantic sea-shore. The big eyes were almost black and her mixed blood gave the whites a smoky tinge. Her features were nilotic with a small, flared nose and a soft, wide mouth that was so full that it looked too swollen to be kissed. Her upper lip would never cover the two gleaming front teeth. My hand could have encompassed the slender neck. She was wearing a thin cotton dress. White, with fringes at the skirt and sleeves, and the fringes jiggled and swung as she walked towards me. So did her beautiful breasts. She was tall and her legs were long. If she had a flaw, it was her feet. They were obviously made for walking.

She sat down, smiling, at my table, and her hand reached across the table to cover mine.

'I pray you come to see me, Johnny.'

'Why?'

'I have something to give you.' The big brown eyes swam with tears and she placed something small, wrapped in thin tissue paper, in front of me.

I opened it slowly and carefully. It was a silver dollar. A Maria Theresa dollar, sharply minted and glinting in the dull light. I looked at her face and she said, '*Seulement a donner de la bonne chance.*'

'Who told you, Maria?'

She shrugged. 'You knew it would happen some day soon. Is best this way.'

'Why?'

'I think he try to be kind, this way.'

'Who?'

'Kanassian. Otherwise he have you killed.'

'He wouldn't dare.'

The big, melting brown eyes looked at my face.

'You don't understand this place, my love. He talk many, many times to have you killed. They never touch him. He is in too many pockets.'

'I'll write to you, sweetie. Will you write to me?'

'If is possible, I write.' She raised the curved eyebrows. 'You want make love with me? Emilio say is OK we use his room.'

I shook my head and leaned across to kiss her. There was a salt taste on her soft mouth. I watched her walk across the dance floor. A wealthy Arab snapped his fingers at her. She ignored him, turned and waved to me, and walked alone into the back room.

I slid the heavy silver coin into my pocket and walked back up the hill, and tried to think of Maria Yassou's feet.

The light was beginning to go as I walked back up to the hotel, and I wondered what the embassy would have said if I'd told them I wanted the consul to arrange for Maria Yassou and me to be married.

Back at the hotel I sold the Lancia by telephone to Dickie Bethell who had long lusted after it. After that there was only the time to pass before I handed over to my successor.

There was enough hot water for a bath and I lay there with my feet on the taps, going through the evidence and clues about Kanassian. There wasn't much that was illegal in the Horn of Africa that he didn't have a hand in. Arms-running, drugs, the black-market were the underpinning of a massive group of quite legal enterprises. Legal if you ignored the murders, the beatings-up, that maintained the monopolies. Blackmail and vice were not local crimes. There was nothing a man could do that would provide blackmail material in Addis. And vice was as normal, and taken for granted, as the sunshine.

All London was concerned with was the virtual certainty that Kanassian was co-operating with the Japanese and the Vichy French who were still hanging on in Madagascar and Djibouti. What they were most concerned with was that Kanassian advised the Emperor himself on his business deals. And if His Imperial Highness's resentment against us for liberating his country could be converted by Kanassian into active but clandestine co-operation

with our enemies, then we should have even bigger problems on
our hands.

I had a meal before I took a taxi. There wasn't much of a crowd
at Kathi Kathiki's place although it was after eleven. A few rich
Greeks and Arabs and a sprinkling of people from the embassy
and the military mission. The word had obviously gone out and
they never quite noticed me.

I was dancing with Kathi when he came in. He was about thirty
and bald at the front. I saw him standing there looking for me.
The band was playing "*J'attendrai*" and Kathi was singing softly
to me in Greek. It sounded very sad.

We sat in a corner and by three o'clock I'd handed over. His
name was Powell. Logan Powell, and he'd been recruited into MI6
from one of those fancy regiments that wear chain-mail on their
shoulders on Mess nights. He had listened, silent and attentive,
as I went over the saga of Kanassian. His questions showed that
he'd grasped most of it first time. He'd got those small eyes that
seem to take everything in without moving about much. I had the
feeling that he would have Kanassian in the bag before long.

I sat there with one last drink and looked at the crowd. They
were the usual bunch. Third Secretaries' wives dancing languor-
ously with attachés, silk scarves draped carelessly across bare
shoulders, trying to lift the image of Kathi's joint out of its primitive
mud. But they could never compete with the pretty Abyssinian girls
dancing with the soldiers, who took it for granted that the sole
purpose of the last waltz was to give their partners an erection.

Powell drove me to the airstrip where the Beechcraft was
waiting.

I was going to miss Addis and the bougainvillaea. And most of
all I was going to miss Maria Yassou.

Command were obviously worried about the situation in Addis.
Other sources were confirming our suspicions. They gave me
truck-loads of rifles and ammunition, a radio link and a couple
of *askaris* from the Camel Corps at Mogadishu, and sent me into
the Ogaden.

The Ogaden is hundreds of square miles of desert and scrub;
its only inhabitants are nomadic Somalis following the annual
rains with their flocks. There were no Europeans there, and no
towns beyond a few ramshackle huts. They dropped food for us
in a weekly parachute drop from a Lysander based at Aden; and
I lived on goats' milk and Kellogg's Corn Flakes.

The reason for sending me there was quite straightforward.

The Ogaden bordered on Ethiopia. Somalis hate Ethiopians. And Somalis love guns and fighting. For the Somalis my trucks and I were living proof that Allah rewards the prayers of good men. All I had to do was to show them how to use the guns and then point them in the right direction. The theory was that with a guerilla war on his south-eastern frontier His Imperial Highness would not only be kept busy, but that he might be bright enough to take the hint that there were more ways than one of skinning a cat. He *was* bright enough and he took the hint.

After that, for me, it was North Africa, Italy and finally Germany. I always meant to find out how Logan Powell had fared in Addis, but I never did.

My demob was held back beyond VE-Day and VJ-Day because the Russians in their zone of Germany looked as if they might be thinking of coming over the border, but I was out by June 1947.

With my Bonnie and Clyde chalk-striped demob suit and my brown trilby hat I tried hard to feel like a civilian. It took time, and there weren't all that many jobs. My letter of recommendation from 21 Army Group said that I was an expert at the penetration of underground movements, and potential employers would shift uneasily behind their desks as they handed the letter back to me.

It took a couple of years before things settled down and I found a niche in advertising. I moved through the various stages from copywriter to group creative head, until finally I had an offer from one of the bigger agencies as creative director.

It was seven years after the war, and I'd been at the agency for a couple of weeks.

She was about thirty, just a bit older perhaps. And full of her own importance. Not pretty, but alert blue eyes and a narrow, stylish face. The kind of face that comes out of Benenden in England or Les Oiseaux in Paris. She stood there in front of my desk, all twin-set and pearls.

'I'm the chairman's secretary and you're Johnny Grant. Yes?'

'Yes.'

She grinned. 'I was brought up on stories about you.'

'Are you sure it was me? I think it must have been some other Johnny Grant.'

'Oh, no. You were in Ethiopia. In Addis. Weren't you?'

'Yes.' I looked up at her face. 'Who are you?'

'I'm Haluk Kanassian's daughter. When I was a young girl he used to tell me about you. My brother and I had bed-time stories about you instead of Hans Andersen.'

'What happened to your father?'

'Nothing. He's still there, but he's an old man now. He really liked you, you know.'

I laughed. 'He must have hated my guts.'

'Oh, no,' she cried. 'He was a fan of yours.' She hesitated and then said, 'Would you like to meet him, he's coming here in two weeks' time?'

I was silent for a few moments and she said, 'He's given a million dollars for a library. For Cambridge. He's coming over to lay the foundation stone. It would make the journey worthwhile if you could come. It really would.'

I looked up at her. 'What's your name?'

'Adele.'

'I'll come if you think he would like it.'

Two days later I received my engraved invitation from one of the Cambridge colleges.

They had put aside a small study off the crowded hall for Kanassian and me. His hair was still mainly black although he must have been around seventy. His welcome was warm and we talked about the days of '41 and '42 like veterans of Agincourt. There were obviously no grudges on either side, but I didn't ask him how he'd managed to keep out of the net that London and I had so carefully woven round him. He offered no explanations, but I knew from the amused look in the brown eyes that he was well aware of my curiosity.

His daughter came in for me after about half an hour.

'Come and meet some of the others.'

She led me over to a couple standing in a corner by one of the stained-glass windows. She said, 'Let me introduce my husband.'

And a smiling Logan Powell held out his hand.

'And Daddy's wife.'

Maria Yassou turned round from the window, and her eyes were wet with tears.

This story was written for the 1980 Mystery Guild Anthology *edited by John Waite.*

For a time during the war I lived in Addis Ababa when my official title was "Military Liaison Officer to the Emperor, Haile Selassie". I expanded this short story into a novel which was published by Grafton in 1982.

After the novel was published I got a nice letter from a man in Cairo who told me that he desperately wanted the address of Aliki. He assured me that his intentions were entirely honourable – he wanted to marry her. I felt a little sad having to write to him to explain that the adorable Aliki was a figment of my imagination.

It was also the start of a long friendship with Detlef Blettenberg, a well-known German thriller writer who at that time lived in Bangkok. There was a nice post-script from his girl-friend, a beautiful Somali girl named Huda. I wish they'd hurry up and get married so that everything's neat and tidy.

DOUBLE GAME

As he reached out his hand for the cup, Anne-Marie noticed again the disjointed fingers that gave the odd claw-like look to his hand. There was a time when she noticed them every day and it had sickened her – not the appearance of his hands but the memory of how they had got that way.

There had been pieces in the papers about the couple who had survived the concentration camps, married and set up a practice as GPs in a London suburb. In anger she had told reporters of how he had intended to be a surgeon until the Nazis had broken his fingers to try and make him talk. But they'd had enough of concentration camp stories. And the couple weren't even Jews – just members of a Resistance group that had been betrayed to the Germans. There'd been no medal on which to hang the story, either.

The group had operated in the Dordogne – successfully – until a couple of months after D-Day when the Gestapo had moved down into the Unoccupied Zone to wipe out the SOE networks. Anne-Marie had ended up in Ravensbrück camp and Johnny had been found, after the surrender, in Mauthausen.

She had realised that people were quite proud of the two war heroes who were now their family doctors; but they didn't want to know the details. There were things the British didn't talk about in public: love, divorce, bravery, cowardice and how much you earned.

Johnny turned now to look at his wife: a handsome woman, rather than beautiful, her thick hair still mainly black with only a dramatic streak of white at each temple. 'Who's on emergency call tonight, sweetie?'

She put down the newspaper. 'Not us, thank heaven. It's Rothman's turn this weekend.' She paused. 'By the way, what did old Raeburn want this morning that he couldn't discuss with me?'

Johnny laughed softly. 'He's got a hernia, poor old boy – not a bad one, but he thought it wasn't right to talk about that sort of thing with a lady.'

'So much for women's lib and all that,' Anne-Marie commented wryly.

'He meant well, sweetie.'

She reached for the newspaper again. 'I was just checking who's on *Desert Island Discs* today.' She turned over the pages to the radio programmes and read aloud. '"6.15. *Desert Island Discs*. Guest: novelist Paul Kempfe." Sounds interesting.' She reached forward and switched on the radio.

Roy Plomley was already giving the introduction. '. . . Our castaway this week is Paul Kempfe – the author whose book *Beyond the Mountain* has been translated into seventeen languages and is currently heading the bestseller lists all over the world.' There was a pause and then he asked, 'Paul – where were you born?'

'I was born in Peine, a small town just outside Hanover. I still live there with my family.'

'Does music mean a lot to you? Do you play a musical instrument?'

'Yes, music means a lot to me – all kinds of music. I play the piano very badly, but my wife plays beautifully and my eldest daughter was a professional violinist before she gave it up to start her own family.'

'Good – now, your first choice.'

'Well, I like both classical music and popular music . . . so I thought I would choose records that would remind me of my life . . . bits of nostalgia. So the first record I have chosen is a Viennese song. It's called "*Sag beim Abschied leise servus*". *Servus* is a very Viennese word that one used to say goodbye to show that you hope to meet that person again.'

As they listened to the song Anne-Marie said, 'Must be fun choosing your eight records.'

'I suppose it is.' He sounded as if his thoughts were far away.

'Are you OK, Johnny? You seem preoccupied.'

'I was just thinking about the chap's voice.'

'Me too. I've heard it before somewhere.'

Roy Plomley was speaking again. '"*Sag beim Abschied*", sung by Peter Alexander. Now, Paul, your bestseller has been translated into English. Where did you learn to speak the language so well?'

'My father was very much an Anglophile. He had a great love for London and the theatre, so he insisted that I learned English at school; and then later I took it at university.'

'You must have been in your early twenties when war broke out – what happened to you then?'

The man's voice was more subdued, slightly tense. 'I wanted to be a fighter pilot in the Luftwaffe but I'm afraid I didn't pass the eyesight test.'

'Why a fighter pilot?'

Paul Kempfe laughed. 'I must have been stupid, I guess. No, I think it was very simple, really – it was just that the fighter pilots got all the pretty girls. But it wasn't for me . . . so I joined the army instead.'

'Where did you serve?'

'Oh, all over the place. You got moved about like a Cook's tour.'

'Let's have your next choice.'

'It's a French song by Josephine Baker – an American who was more French than the French themselves. I've chosen her singing "*J'ai deux amours*".'

As the record started they looked at each other and Anne-Marie said softly, 'You were right, Johnny: you do know who he is – Patrice.'

There was a long silence and then Johnny whispered, 'The lousy bastard. "The Germans" must have known every move we made.'

'That record, the voice . . . the facts all fit.'

It seemed incredible that Patrice was a German – and a traitor. Patrice, the Frenchman who was always encouraging and optimistic when things were tough, who amused them all because he was in love with Josephine Baker and that song. He'd played the record until it was almost worn out and Johnny had asked London to include a new one with their next supplies drop.

'Can we find out where he's staying?' Anne-Marie asked.

'His publishers will have put him up at a big hotel. I'll ring round. By God, I owe it to the others to find him.'

That evening Johnny knocked on the door of Room 703 of the Hilton, Anne-Marie by his side.

'Good evening, Patrice,' Johnny said quietly as the door was opened. 'It's been a long time.'

Paul Kempfe stood in the doorway, looking puzzled. He was still an impressive man, handsome and tall. The black hair was strikingly white now, making him look less French, more German. 'I don't understand,' he was saying.

'You do, my friend. You remember me – Johnny Parsons. And I'm sure you remember my wife – Anne-Marie.'

The shock on the German's face was obvious. 'I see . . . you'd better come in . . .' He pointed to the large settee. 'Why don't you sit down? I didn't want to come here but I had to. My publishers insisted. I made a dozen excuses, but in the end I had to come.'

'Why did you do it?'

'I told you, my publishers . . .'

Johnny cut him short. 'Why did you sell us down the river? Why *did* you do it, for God's sake?'

'I had no choice. I was an officer in the Abwehr. I spoke French fluently and I was told to penetrate SOE. It was an order.'

'You could have come over to us. You could have told us, and we'd have got you out.'

'But why should I? I was fighting for Germany. You killed Germans.'

'I didn't torture them. I didn't send them to extermination camps. I didn't . . .'

'Is that what happened to you?'

'You know damn well it did. Don't pretend that you didn't know what your thugs did to the SOE people that they captured.'

Patrice shook his head slowly. 'Once you were arrested I was withdrawn. I played no part in what happened after your arrest.'

'You knew what had happened to the others you betrayed before.'

'OK, I knew – but not in detail. I wasn't in the Gestapo. Certainly the Abwehr didn't go in for brutality.'

'No, my friend – you let the others do the dirty work for you.'

Paul Kempfe sighed sadly. 'Why did you come here to see me?'

Very slowly and with great relish Johnny told him: 'To make sure that it was you before we expose you. We shall tell the whole media that, apart from being a bestselling writer, you caused the torture and death of a great many people.'

Paul Kempfe didn't even protest. 'How did you know I was Patrice?'

'We heard you on the radio – your voice, your answers ... and the record you chose, of course.'

Patrice nodded and half-smiled. 'Ah yes, "*J'ai deux amours*" – of course, you always pulled my leg for playing it so often ... once too often, it seems.'

Anne-Marie spoke for the first time, her voice firm. 'You must have known that what you did would catch up with you some day.'

'As a matter of fact I never did think that. When the war ended, Germany was a shambles. I moved to Göttingen and worked as a teacher for several years. I met my wife, we married and had children, then I started writing my novels – and 1943 seemed far away.' He paused. 'And so it's your turn now to wound people – my wife, my children ...'

'Why not, Patrice?'

'Because I didn't *choose* the part I had to play. When the war started, it was discovered that because of my French mother I spoke the language fluently and I was recruited into the Abwehr. They weren't thugs, you know – most of them weren't even party members. Admittedly we all wanted Germany to win the war – I don't pretend otherwise. Maybe I was naive or stupid – but I don't think I was evil. I didn't understand what war was, where it could lead us, but it's like a moving staircase – once you are on it, you can't get off.

'When I was ordered to penetrate SOE I knew that if my cover was blown I would be killed. I do not deny that because of me, men and women died; but the same is true of you. Did it never worry you that SOE was causing the death of so many French men and women?'

Johnny looked grave. 'I tried not to let it happen. When it did, I bitterly regretted that patriots were being tortured and killed.'

'But it didn't stop you doing it, did it, any more than it stopped me?'

'True – but there is one big difference between us: nobody says prayers every night for me to burn in hell.'

Patrice said softly, 'You mean people do that about me?'

'I mean that there are widows, sons, daughters who would kill you if they knew.'

'And you, Johnny?'

'Me too. I'd like to see you hang.'

'And you, Anne-Marie? Would you like to see me hang?'

'I couldn't answer that, Patrice. But I know what Johnny means.

I understand because I'm part of it. You were able to walk away and eventually forget it. We couldn't – we were left with scars that wouldn't heal, that won't ever heal.

'Johnny ought to have been a surgeon, but just look at the joints of his fingers. When they broke them they were never re-set. Concentration camps didn't waste time on people who were going to be gassed. When he came out, it was too late. I married a man who I know is brave, so it breaks my heart when he screams in the night – not just way back but now, still. I see him lying there, trembling . . .' She paused. 'D'you remember René?'

'The one with the beard and the girl at the garage?'

'That's the one. You know what happened to him? He was sent to Buchenwald. When he got out of the Allies' Hospital the war had been over for nearly a year. They tried to break it to him gently that the girl from the garage had been arrested by your people. She was sent to Ravensbrück. She was young and pretty and they put her in the camp brothel. She never came out of the camp. Nobody ever found out what had happened to her.

'René went to see her parents, to comfort them and get comfort for himself. They cursed him and blamed him for her death. The whole village hated him. Three days after he came back, he hanged himself.'

She paused and then went on, 'Pierre, who got hold of that gramophone for you, came back from his camp. He seemed OK at first but then he started going every day to the railway bridge where they picked us up that night. In the end they put him in the hospice for the mentally sick at Angoulême. He's still in there now. Do you want to hear more? There is more to tell.'

Patrice shook his head and said quietly, 'No. That's more than enough.' After a while he said, 'Tell me; tell me about you two.'

'We don't have a family, Patrice – because of what happened to me in Ravensbrück.'

'And telling the newspapers will put that right?'

'It will square the account.'

'I am truly sorry for what happened to all those people but, looking back, I can see how young we all were – and idealistic. I think our superiors on both sides cashed in on that – made what we were doing seem rather romantic: a game, knights in armour. My people warned me that if I was caught I should be killed, your people probably told you the same. But neither of us actually expected it to happen. It will seem crazy to you but, even while we've been talking here tonight, I wished you could meet my wife and children and we could talk about old times as if we were just old opponents, not killers.'

'You're right, my friend, it does seem crazy. It wasn't a game; it was a war. My people paid the bill for your betrayal and now it's your turn. Come on, Anne-Marie. Let's go.'

At midnight she sat on the edge of the bed, watching her husband. The misshapen fingers were clenching and unclenching. 'Do you honestly see it doing any good, Johnny?' she said at last.

'Yes. It'll do me good.'

'That's not like you.' She stroked his hand gently. 'Before we met him I felt exactly as you did. But while we were talking to him my mind went back to those times in France. He somehow belonged there with us, no matter if he did shop us in the end. You were twenty-two, Johnny, and he was what? Twenty-four, twenty-five. We had guts, but we were terribly naive. We were playing games, dangerous games – especially him. If we had discovered what he was up to, we would have torn him to pieces and thought nothing of it . . . but not now, Johnny, not now. It would do nothing – absolutely nothing. His wife would suffer, his children, his mother. But nothing would change for us or for René or the others.'

'For God's sake, are you suggesting letting him go scot free?' Johnny demanded, aghast.

'He won't go scot free. He's got imagination, he'll remember – whether he likes it or not. He listened to every terrible word we said.' She paused, remembering the past. 'You know, when you ran the network and I was the radio-operator, there were times when people did stupid things against your orders – things that could have led to us all being captured. Remember René and the girl from the garage? He took all sorts of awful risks to see her. You nearly always reprimanded them very quietly and sent them on their way. I asked you once why you didn't do more about their disobedience. Can you remember what you said?'

'No. I don't remember anything about it.'

'You said, "He's just a man, sweetie. If I destroy his confidence he'll only be half a man – and maybe, on occasions, making love to a girl is more important than winning a war and it doesn't take as long!" I thought that was pretty good for a twenty-two-year-old. It seemed like a big mind, not a small one. I feel about Patrice like you felt about your people. Let's leave him in peace, Johnny.'

61

'And René? And all the others?'

'Let them rest, Johnny. Let them rest in peace. Let me phone him and tell him that it's not his and his family's turn to be destroyed.'

For the first time since he'd heard Patrice's voice that morning, the tension in Johnny eased. 'Is that what you really want, sweetie?'

'Yes – and it's what you really want, too. You've just got a bit put out of joint thinking about those days again. You're a healer, not a destroyer, Johnny.'

He sighed and reached for the light switch. 'OK – you do it, love, not me.'

He was aware of her getting out of bed before she said, 'I'll ring him now. I don't suppose he can sleep, either.'

Anne-Marie woke her husband at eleven the next morning. 'We've had a letter,' she told him. 'It must have been put through the letterbox during the night.'

'Probably the bill from the paper shop.'

'It isn't. It's from Patrice, Paul Kempfe – I'll read it to you . . .'

Dear friends,

I found your address in the telephone directory, and I am writing to thank you for deciding to spare me – and, more importantly, my wife and children. Your attitude to us is generous and civilised. I've been thinking all night about what we said, and wondering. You accused me of betrayal; yet *not* to have told my superiors about you would have been a worse betrayal. Let me try to explain.

My father was German; my mother French. I liked my father very much. I admired him. With my mother it was different – I *loved* her. She seemed a very romantic person when I was a boy; she played the piano and sang – always French songs, little songs. For me she *was* France – a place where the sun always shone, where the flowers – poppies, cornflowers, marigolds – always bloomed brighter, where there was constant laughter. I'd spend the long summer holidays in her family's château. But term-time, real life, was Hanover. I was born a *German*, Johnny, and it was my duty to serve the country of my birth, not that of my heart. Britain was our enemy. You had declared war on us, remember – not us on you. And the French Resistance was aiding you against Germany. It pained me to hand over my French comrades to the Gestapo; but to have failed to do so would have been to betray my true country – and I was, and am, a patriot.

Just before the war ended I was given a medal. It seems that Berlin was more generous than London to its secret agents. It wasn't awarded for my time in France so I hope you will understand when I send it to you, Johnny – just as a keepsake, as a token of appreciation.

I will write to you again when I get back home but I shall understand if you don't reply. You've been generous enough already.

When you were with me last night, I felt as if I was Patrice again, not, Yours sincerely,

Paul Kempfe.

Silently Johnny opened the small box enclosed in the envelope. 'It's a Knight's Cross with oak leaves and crossed swords,' he whispered. 'The highest order of the Iron Cross.'

'So you got a medal after all, my love.' Anne-Marie smiled. 'Better late than never.'

This came from being on Desert Island Discs *myself when it was still Roy Plomley's show. I was aware that in choosing the records in a short and superficial run over one's life that there is inevitably a kind of bending of the facts.*

Most of my current listening pleasure comes from classical music. Cello and violin concertos and all that. But way back my listening was Harry Roy, Ambrose, Lew Stone, Roy Fox and Al Bowlly. It seemed that whatever I chose I would seem deceptive. If I chose classical stuff people who knew me way back would think I was trying to look more discerning than I really was. And those who know me now would think I was trying to look like the poor boy from the back streets of Birmingham. I thought, to hell with it – and chose the stuff from the old days. I still like it and after all you don't have to exclude one to have the other. Even in the chat between the records about one's life there's the hope that you might end up looking wiser or more interesting than you really are. Haven't writers got devious minds?

The story was first published by Woman's Own *in 1985.*

THE OTHER KIND OF TREASON

She switched off the radio. Phone-ins were such rubbish but they were company if you were on your own. All those idiot men airing their monotonous views on violence at football matches and cranky women going on about how much money the Queen got a year. It was Friday night and no office for two whole days. She could almost hear her mother saying what she always used to say – "Friday night's Amami night". She slid off her shoes and walked through to the kitchen. The door-bell rang as she reached into the fridge for the strawberry yoghurt.

She could see the silhouette of a man's head and shoulders through the glass panes and she kept the chain on the door as she opened it.

'Mrs Judith Howard?'

'Yes.'

'I wonder if I could have a word with you?'

'What about?'

'About your ex-husband.'

'Who are you?'

'I'm a police officer, Mrs Howard. Superintendent Collett. Here's my identity card.'

He pushed a leather wallet through the door opening and she switched on the hall light to look at it. There was a photograph under cellophane on the left-hand side and on the other side it gave his name and number with a stamp saying that it was issued from New Scotland Yard. There was a broad red diagonal from corner to corner. And in white on the diagonal it said "Special Branch". It looked official enough, but how could you tell? She

65

slid off the chain and opened the door to look at him. He looked pleasant enough but he looked very young. They said it was a sign of growing old when policemen started looking young.

She handed back the wallet and as he slid it into his jacket pocket she noticed the clip-board tucked under his arm.

He smiled. 'If you'd like to check you could ring your local police station. They know I'm calling on you.'

'No. That's all right. You'd better come in.'

She showed him into the living-room and pointed to one of the armchairs. She heard it creak as he lowered his big body into what had once been Ian's chair. She wondered fleetingly if the sherry she still had from Christmas was OK. Did sherry go off after four months?

She sat down opposite him and waited for him to speak.

'When did you last see your husband . . . your ex-husband, Mrs Howard?'

She had a vision of the picture on the wall at school. The small boy in velvet clothes, standing on a stool, surrounded by Cromwell's Roundheads. And the title "When did you last see your father?"

'Are you OK, Mrs Howard?'

She shook her head to collect her thoughts. 'Yes, I'm sorry. What did you say?'

'I asked you when you last saw Mr Howard.'

'About two months ago. He called for some of his books.'

'Can you remember the date?'

'No. It was February or March. There was still snow on the ground.'

'You've not seen him since then?'

'No.' She paused and looked at him. 'What is all this? Has Ian done something?'

He looked at her quizzically. 'What do you think he might have done?'

'I've no idea.'

'He's at Wormwood Scrubs at the moment. Held for questioning.'

'But what about?'

'If I told you that your ex-husband was under suspicion of being involved in espionage, would you be surprised?'

The shock on her face was obvious and genuine. 'Of course I'd be surprised. I wouldn't believe it, anyway.'

'Why not?'

'He didn't like the Russians.'

Collett raised his eyebrows. 'I didn't say what country he was suspected of spying for.' He paused. 'Why did you assume it was the Soviet Union?'

She shrugged. 'It always is, isn't it? Who else could it be?'

'What sort of man was he?'

'For heaven's sake, who can say what sort of man somebody is? Could your wife say what sort of man you are?'

He smiled. 'I'm not married yet.' His eyes looked intently at her face. 'Would you say he was a truthful man, or did he tell lies?'

'He told lies sometimes. Most people do.'

'What did he tell lies about?'

'Pretending to be working when he was with other women.'

'Did that happen often?'

'Often enough for me to divorce him.'

Collett looked at her intently. 'I read through your divorce petition. You didn't actually provide any proof of those relationships.'

'Maybe you'd consider a pair of girl's panties in his briefcase just a coincidence.'

'From your petition it looked as if you kept a diary of those occasions when he was working late or out of town, didn't you? That was part of your evidence, wasn't it?'

'Yes.'

'Do you still have that diary?'

'No. I burnt it.'

'Why did you destroy it?'

'Because it disgusted me.'

'You didn't tackle him about these – infidelities – until just before you instructed your solicitor. How did he react when you confronted him?'

'He was very angry at first. Really angry. Accused me of spying on him. Said I was jumping to conclusions. That there was no other woman.'

'Was he usually given to anger?'

'No. He was a very quiet, calm man.'

He looked at his notes. 'And roughly a week later you discovered the underclothing in his briefcase?'

'Yes.'

'And you tackled him again?'

'No. I went straight to my solicitor. I'd had enough.'

'Do you regret divorcing him?' Collett leaned back in the chair.

She hesitated and then shook her head. 'No. I wasn't happy with him.'

'Why not?'

'I don't really know. He didn't love me, I knew that. And as time went by I realised I didn't love him, either.'

'If I told you that there were no other women, ever, would you be surprised?'

'I wouldn't believe you.'

'You wouldn't believe me if I said that those times you assumed he was being unfaithful he was actually meeting the KGB officer who directed him.'

'Do KGB men wear lacy panties?'

He half-smiled. 'When you first tackled him he could have been scared that you knew about what he had actually been doing. Maybe the panties were just to make sure that you went on thinking it was other women. By the way, did he have a camera?'

She shook her head. 'I never saw one.'

'You said that you knew he didn't love you. Was he violent towards you or anything like that?'

'Of course he wasn't. He wasn't that sort of man.'

'Did he have many friends?'

'None so far as I know.'

He nodded. 'These people can't afford to have friends. They have to be loners.'

'Or maybe it's the other way round.'

Collett looked interested. 'I don't understand.'

'Maybe loners who can't get on with people look for friendship or contact in other ways.'

He noticed that there were tears in her eyes and he picked up his clip-board from the floor and stood up.

'Well . . . thank you for your help, Mrs Howard. I'll leave my card and if you think of anything that might be significant, perhaps you'd contact me.'

She didn't answer but she stood up and showed him to the door, watching as he walked down the short path to the Rover parked under the street-lamp.

The photographs were in a chocolate box. A box of Black Magic that he'd bought for her the second time they went out.

There was the set of four that they'd done at Charing Cross Station; the bottom right-hand one had been cut out. It was a handsome face. Black wavy hair. Big brown eyes and a full sensuous mouth and that cleft in his chin like Kirk Douglas. But it was a solemn face. A sad face.

There was a faded black and white picture of a group of small boys and girls. Five years old. It had been taken at the orphanage where he had been brought up, on an outing to Yarm. The same solemn face as he stood there in the rumpled jersey at the far edge of the group. There was a snap taken of him in his RAF uniform in front of a Lancaster. He was a sergeant-navigator then. And there was a press photograph cut out from the local paper of prisoners newly released from Changi Camp at Singapore. His arms and legs were like sticks and the thin skin was puckered over his ribs. There had been other photographs but those were the only ones she had kept after the big clear-out when the divorce came through. As she pushed the chocolate box back into the drawer of the sideboard she switched on the radio and then burst into tears, her hands to her face.

A few minutes later she was washing her face in the bathroom. As she looked at her face in the mirror she wondered what it would be like for a man like him to be in prison. The policeman hadn't said what he was supposed to have done. It sounded as if they thought he was a spy or a mole, or whatever they called them these days. For a moment she thought of going out for a meal or perhaps going round to her mother's. But she hated eating on her own in a café, and her mother would be no comfort. She had always disliked Ian right from when she first took him home. She never liked anyone for long. There had been a barrage of criticism behind his back. He was old enough to be her father. He was stuck-up and full of his own importance. Her mother was given to unerring misjudgments of people. The new miracle doctor was a quack six months later and the honest greengrocer who saved her the good tomatoes was suspected of giving short weight before the year was out. She always managed to see people's virtues as vices and, inevitably, her outrageous criticisms made you defend people you didn't really like.

She warmed up a TV dinner and watched the nine o'clock news. The play was about old people in a home and she leaned forward and switched channels. A documentary on open-heart surgery and a discussion group on abortion were the other choices and she switched off the set.

He'd sworn there was no other woman but she hadn't believed him. She felt ashamed now at what her thoughts had been about those panties. She had built up a mental picture of a pretty young blonde. Much younger than her and with all that pushiness that girls had today. Blue eyes and a tight sweater and high-heeled shoes. She wondered what she would have done if he had told her the truth. She had threatened him with divorce and she could tell that he was upset about it. But was he upset about a divorce, or that she might know what he was up to? Or maybe both? Maybe he hadn't loved her the way she would have liked, but he was never unkind. He bothered about her when she wasn't well. He took her out on Friday nights and came shopping with her on Saturday mornings. There weren't many husbands who'd do that. And he'd appreciated the things she did for him. The cooking, the washing and ironing, and he was always saying how nicely she kept the place. She had only come to appreciate those things now that she didn't have them any more.

She sighed. Maybe she'd been too hasty. Maybe she'd just used the women as an excuse when it was really his aloofness that had been the real thing. The policeman had said he was a loner. But he'd never had a chance of being anything else. He hated talking about it, but she'd got it out of him bit by bit when they were courting. And always his eyes had been watching her face to see if she was rejecting him because of what he told her.

He was illegitimate and the succession of "uncles" who lived with his mother had hated his guts. He was four years old when one of them had broken his jaw and an arm and he had been taken to the hospital. He even remembered the man's name after all those years. "Uncle" Jamie. Jamie Maclaren. From the hospital he had been sent to the orphanage in Sunderland.

At the orphanage he had been fed and clothed, and educated after a fashion. He said that they hadn't been unkind but he'd hated the fact that he was just one among hundreds. He'd always wanted to be special. He'd had dreams about a mother who cuddled him and a father who bought him a train set and a bicycle. He'd smiled when he told her about the dreams. But it was a sad, uncertain smile. Once she'd joked and said that she'd buy him a train set and a bicycle. He'd put his arms round her and rested his head on her shoulder as she stroked his neck, and it was only then that she realised how deep those old wounds had gone.

He said quite openly that he didn't want friends. He didn't trust anybody, he'd said. It was a waste of time. Sooner or later they'd let you down. And that was a thought she didn't like. Maybe she too had let him down. Accused him of something he hadn't done when it was impossible for him to prove that it wasn't true by telling her what he really had been doing on those nights and missing weekends. Maybe she was as much a traitor as he was. A traitor to him. If she hadn't thought it was other women and hadn't accused him, they would still be married. She wouldn't be sitting alone with a TV dinner and a blank TV screen. And maybe he wouldn't be in prison.

For three days she wondered what she could do to help him. Nobody else would help him. She phoned Superintendent Collett at the number he had given her and asked if she could talk to him again. He arranged to come and see her that evening.

She had tidied the place up anxiously. Just like her mother when the doctor was coming. Patting cushions, moving a chair a couple of inches, putting a copy of the *Radio Times* and the *Guardian* on the coffee table. He came exactly on time and when he was seated comfortably she told him of Ian Howard's sad childhood and the effect that it had on his personality. When she had finished he looked at her face.

'What prompted you to tell me all this, Mrs Howard?'

She sighed and shrugged nervously. 'I think I felt guilty about causing him to be in prison. Jumping to the wrong conclusions.'

'You mean about other women?'

'Yes.'

'We should have pulled him in, anyway. He's been under surveillance for a long time. It wasn't you who made him work for the Russians.'

'What did he do for them?'

'Officially I can't tell you . . . off the record, he's been passing them all the technical information they wanted on the electronics that his employers produce for the Ministry of Defence. Almost all of it was Top Secret.'

'How long has he been doing this?'

'He's been under suspicion for two years but he's been doing it for just over eight years.'

'But it was me that made him panic.'

'Maybe. But I shouldn't worry about it, Mrs Howard. I think you'll find he's capable of looking after himself.'

'I feel so ashamed that I didn't trust him.'

He smiled as he stood up. 'I'd say you had been a very good wife.' As he shook her hand he said, 'It'll be in the papers in a few days' time but there'll be no mention of you.'

'Won't the reporters trace me?'

'I don't think so. We shan't mention that he was married and there's other things they'll be more interested in.'

It was in the Friday papers, right on the front pages; and for her it was like a bomb. There were long columns of text but no mention of her. But the blow was in the two photographs and their caption. There was one of Ian being led to a police car and the other, alongside it, was of a very pretty girl. Blonde and smiling. It said she was twenty-six, her name was Anna Gavrilova – she had been Ian Howard's KGB contact. She had been declared persona non grata by the Foreign Office and had left the country two months ago to return to Moscow. Her cover job had been as archivist at the Soviet Embassy. She remembered again what he had said so often. Never trust anybody.

When, as an Intelligence officer, I had to arrest people, it often angered and saddened me that so many other people were hurt in the process. Wives, children, parents and friends. Of course there were sometimes wives who "shopped" their husbands, but there were far more who knew nothing about what their man had been up to. And it was these, the survivors, who had to get on with their lives. Easy targets for derision or revenge and always touched with irrational guilt that somehow they were responsible for what had happened. The children suffered too.

This story was first published in Women's Realm *in 1984.*

JUST AN ORDINARY WOMAN

It was the last item on TVS's local news. The girl newsreader spoke over the pictures. 'At the inquest at Hastings today on the death of the woman known only as Mary, the verdict was that she died of natural causes.' The picture showed a bulldozer demolishing a rough wooden hut in a clearing in a wood, and the commentary continued, 'It is only ten days since the council demolished Mary's rough home where she had lived for several years alone.' There was a full-face shot of an elderly woman's face with unkempt hair and a sallow complexion that emphasised her big, sad, dark eyes. '. . . The council spokesman said that exceptions could not be made to the planning laws and Mary had been offered alternative accommodation.' The camera moved in on the announcer's face. 'The police have asked for anyone who could give any information on the dead woman's identity to phone them on Hastings four – two – five – zero – zero – zero.'

The woman sitting watching the TV reached forward and switched off the set. 'Poor soul,' she said, 'what a way to end your life.' She turned to her husband. 'Why do people want to live like that, Joe?'

The old man shrugged. 'Who knows, love? They're obviously escaping from something or somebody. They've had enough of the world.' He sighed and shrugged. 'Maybe they just want to be left alone.'

All she could remember of the first day was getting out of the railway waggon and walking along the platform holding her mother's hand. The station sign said "Oświęcim" and she heard

73

people saying that it was some kind of work-camp run by the Germans. There were hundreds of others, standing beside the high barbed-wire fence, and SS men shouting and hitting people with sticks and batons. It was dark when they finally went through the big gates. For the first time in her life she saw her mother crying.

Albert wasn't handsome but even at fifty he still had a fresh complexion and a boyish face. And he was a kind man in most ways. A lot of neighbourhood women envied her and wondered how she'd got such a husband. They seldom went out. Once a month to the cinema if the film was suitable and even then they went to the matinée performance. She was nineteen when they met at a dance at St Joseph's. He had been staying with his mother for his two weeks' annual holiday from the insurance company in London where he worked as a clerk. She spoke terrible English in those days and he was amused, and obviously taken with the mistakes that she made. But it was kindly done and before long it was more loving than kindness.

She realised right from the start that she had a determined enemy in his mother. It wasn't open warfare. Just a subtle drawing of attention to the fact that she was Polish. A foreigner who couldn't be expected to fit into English ways. But what did it matter, she was only his friend, wasn't she? You had to meet all sorts of people, but it was a pity that she had no relations to guide her on how to behave in a strange country. Obviously her mother was no help to her, was she? So silent and unsmiling. She wondered aloud how they managed to live with the mother employed as an office cleaner. But she'd heard that the German government paid them some sort of pension for their time in prison. When Albert pointed out that in fact they had been in a concentration camp, not a prison, she shrugged and muttered about no smoke without fire. They must have done something or they wouldn't have been put there. Nobody put people in prisons for nothing.

Albert had had a few girl-friends but they had all been put off by his mother's insidious criticisms. And Albert wasn't a great catch, anyway. Not lively enough for most young girls. He didn't play football or go to pubs and he never made passes at them. They liked his affectionate nature but he wasn't a go-getter. In fact, some of them thought, he was a bit of a Jessie – a mother's boy. After they were married she had heard from two or three of his ex-girlfriends that he'd never even kissed them.

By the time she was twenty-one she wasn't just pretty, she was beautiful. The big, dark, heavy-lidded eyes, the neat turned-up nose and the soft, full mouth gave her the look of a Pre-Raphaelite painting. Men at the offices where she worked as a clerk were a little in awe of the withdrawn young beauty. She was invited out by many of them but she always refused. When other girls asked her why she never had dates she shrugged and said that she wasn't interested.

When Albert was promoted to deputy office manager they earned enough between them to get married. And when her mother offered them the ground floor of their rented house it seemed like a sign that they should go ahead.

The night Albert broke the good news to his mother he had had to call out the doctor in the middle of the night. She had complained of being unable to breathe and palpitations in her heart. The doctor had examined her and prescribed capsules that he told Albert, when they were alone, were just tranquillisers. He was an elderly man and had long experience of Albert's mother and her palpitations. It was a common complaint in mothers of only sons who decided to spread their wings.

Albert had insisted that they stuck to all their plans for the wedding. Albert's mother had been too poorly to attend, but her mother and a neighbour had signed as witnesses at the Registrar's office and they had all had lunch at the Kardomah before the couple went off for their three-day honeymoon at Hastings. They came back to their new home and settled in quite easily.

She was thankful that Albert was an undemanding lover and she realised that it was a part of married life that he preferred to ignore. But she recognised early on that Albert was very jealous of any contact she had with other men. Tradesmen who were over-jolly, acquaintances who complimented her on her good looks made him very angry. But it was easy to put such people in their places to please him.

He had been frightened the first time that she had one of her nightmares. She hadn't told him what she had dreamed about and it wasn't a frequent occurrence. There was a railway-siding running along the end of the garden to a gas-works and sometimes the coke waggons made that clanging noise and there was the sound of men shouting. She tried not to notice it but sometimes when she was tired she could hear it echoing in her mind even when everywhere was silent.

*

She had been cleaning the toilets in the hospital hut when the *Kapo*, who was a Hungarian, told her that her mother was on the list. When she'd asked him what list he seemed surprised. Women were wanted for a new set of surgical experiments. He told her that most women didn't survive the repeated operations. She had spoken to the younger of the two doctors, begging him to help and get her mother's name off the list. He had asked her why he should do what she wanted. And all she could say was that her father had been killed by the SS in Warsaw and her mother was all she had left in the world. And she loved her mother. He had made no promises but he'd listened and noted down her mother's name and camp number.

But it was the older doctor who had sent one of the guards for her that evening.

It was six years before Albert's mother gave up the struggle. She invited them to Sunday dinner. After that there were regular visits and their lives assumed the simple routines that were typical of their suburban neighbours. There had never been any question of children. They both had their reasons, although they never discussed them. Albert couldn't face the responsibility of children and the girl, or woman as she was now, couldn't wipe out the horrors of what had happened to children in the death-camp.

So life went on. Some would have thought it monotonous and boring but they found it satisfactory. Neither of them had any wish for excitement and for both of them the routines were their security.

It was Albert who had shown her the short piece in the evening paper that mentioned Auschwitz and its gas chambers. She had pushed the paper away and had refused to read it. She hadn't had one of her nightmares for over two years and she didn't want to do anything that could bring them back.

The living-room in the Hampstead house was a reflection of the man's success and personality. There were black and white photographic enlargements on the walls rather than paintings. Photographs by Ansel Adams, Ernst Haas and Joel Meyerowitz. Leather couches and armchairs, plain white walls and carpets from Turkey and Iran.

There was a coal fire burning in the grate and Stein himself sat facing the two other men. Stein was one of the most respected and successful lawyers specialising in international law. He tossed the butt of his cigar into the fire and then looked back at the older of the two men.

He said softly, 'Why come to me if you won't take my advice?'

The young man interrupted and said harshly, 'My father and mother died in that camp, Mr Stein.'

Stein had lost fourteen close relatives in one camp or another but he knew from long experience that emotion and the law were not a good mixture. He said quietly, 'I was a prosecutor at the Nuremberg trials, my friend. Courts are for the law, not for revenge.'

The older man sighed. 'We are quite sure that he is the man. We have a photograph showing him in SS uniform and a press photograph taken two months ago. They are clearly the same man.'

'And the defence would bring photographic specialists and physiognomists to prove that they were not the same man. Even documentary evidence could be put forward that the man had never been in a camp or in the SS.'

'So what do we need, David, to get him into court?'

Stein smiled. 'That's better. First you need sworn evidence of what you claim your suspect did. Dates, names, facts. Then you need at least two witnesses. People who were in the camp who will testify that their man is the man you say he is. Then evidence of what he did. Not hearsay but eye-witness evidence. And you need to check on your witnesses. Were they there? Are their names on any camp rolls? Tattoo numbers.' He paused. 'When you've got all that, come and see me again.'

The committee had sent them three names and their last known addresses. One was dead and the other was a man of seventy-nine. He was still working as a cutter for one of the better London tailors. Still mentally alert but not happy discussing his life in Auschwitz. They had shown him the two photographs and he'd looked at them for a long time.

'That's Busch, all right. In his uniform. But I'm not sure about this one. Faces change, you know. And it's a long time ago.'

'Do you have contact with any other survivors from those days?'

The old man shook his head. 'It wasn't a school, my friends. We don't have reunions, you know. We try to forget it. All of it.' He sighed. 'Sometimes I ain't even sure it really happened.' His lips quivered and he said quietly, 'I don't want to think about it.'

'Would you testify in court if it was necessary?'

He shook his head. 'No. I've had enough of all that. I still have nightmares about it.'

'Aren't you interested in due punishment for a man who is known to be responsible for the deaths of thousand of innocent people? Don't those people deserve a small effort from you?'

'I'll think about it.'

'We have another name we'd like to contact . . .' the man checked his list, '. . . it's a Mrs Felinska. Jadwiga Felinska. Do you remember that name?'

'Yeah. I remember her. She was a Pole like me.' He frowned. 'I think she had a kid.'

'How come you remember her name?'

'She lived in Wiejska Street in Warsaw. About four doors from where I lived.'

'Have you seen her since the war?'

'Ain't seen nobody. Don't want to neither. You people don't understand, do you? We want to forget.' He pointed angrily at the inside of his wrist and the two men saw the scar where the tattooed number had been removed. 'You people just stir things up. You weren't in the camps. You should leave us alone. Catch these people yourself, if that's what you want.'

'You think they should go unpunished?'

Tears poured down the old man's face and his voice quavered as he said, 'I don't know what I think. Just leave me alone.'

The older man said quietly, 'Thanks for talking to us, Mr Rabinowitz. I'm sorry we had to disturb you.'

It was the young man who called at the house and it was Albert who answered the door.

'Good morning. I'm looking for Mrs Felinska. I understand she lives here.'

'Mrs Felinska died seven years ago.'

'I'm sorry to hear that. Did she have any children, do you know?'

'She had a daughter. She's my wife.'

'I see.' He paused. 'Would it be possible for me to have a word with her?'

'What about?'

'It's a personal matter.'

'About what?'

'I'd rather talk to your wife, sir, if I may.'

'Then the answer is no. You may not.'
And Albert stepped back and slammed the door in his face.

The two men briefed the young woman carefully. They had decided it would be better if it was a woman who made the enquiries. She was to pose as a journalist doing a piece for a magazine about survivors from the Holocaust.

The first interview had been with a neighbour who lived two houses away. She'd been invited in and given a cup of tea. Journalists, like doctors, were unusual visitors and treated accordingly.

'What sort of lady is she?'

'Very reserved. Neither of them is a real neighbour, at all. Keep themselves to themselves.' She smiled. 'She's very ordinary. You couldn't tell her from the rest of us. I've spoken to her a few times at the paper shop but that's about all.'

'Did you know that she'd been in a concentration camp?'

'Not till you told me. I don't really know much about those sort of things.'

'How old is she?'

'I don't really know. In her fifties, I'd think.'

'D'you remember her mother?'

'Oh, yes. She was a nice lady. Couldn't speak English hardly at all. But she always had a smile when she saw you.'

'Did she have many friends?'

'I think she knew Mrs Hargreaves at the grocery quite well and there was Mrs Perrins at the Post Office. That's all I know of.'

'And the daughter's been married for a long time, I understand.'

'They were married before we moved here.'

'What's her husband like?'

The woman smiled. 'That's Albert. He's a quiet one, too.' She laughed. 'He was always a bit possessive. Touchy about her talking to other men. The milkman used to crack a joke with her sometimes and Albert threatened him. Not that I can see Albert raising his fist to anyone. They're very fond of one another. Not many women of over fifty have jealous husbands these days.'

'Has he had any grounds for being jealous, do you think?'

'No. Never. I'd stake me life on it. She was very pretty when she was younger, but no . . . Albert has always been the only one. Not like with some around here I could tell you about.'

She had interviewed five local women and one tradesman and the opinions were all the same. She was a very ordinary lady. Just like the rest of them.

The older man had waited in the car until he'd seen Albert go off to work at his usual time, and then he'd walked up the short path to the porch at the front of the house and rung the bell.

The woman who answered the door had a calm face. She was a little on the stout side but her hair was still black.

'Mrs Cash?'

'Yes.'

'I wonder if I could have a word with you?'

'What about?'

'I'm a member of a committee in London investigating war-crimes. And I think perhaps you could assist us.'

'I think you must be mistaking me for somebody else. I had nothing to do with the war.'

'Your unmarried name was Maria Kristina Felinska, was it not?'

'Yes,' she said quietly. 'How did you know that?'

'From the camp records at Auschwitz – Oświęcim.'

He saw the anxiety in her eyes as she said, 'You'd better come in.'

She led him into the small front room, deftly taking off the covers from the three-piece suite before pointing to one of the armchairs and then sitting down herself. She turned to look at him squarely, her chin lifted, her face tense, no longer calm. And the fingers of one hand picked at a place where the arm of the chair had worn through.

'What is it you want?'

'Do you recognise this man?' He handed her the photograph of the man in his SS uniform. She looked at it for a long time and then she said quietly, 'Who is he?'

'I want you to tell me if you recognise him. I don't want to influence you in any way.'

'There were over a hundred SS-men in the KZ. How could I remember one?'

'This is another picture of the same man, taken a few months ago at the door of his house in Edinburgh. Do you recognise him in that photo, perhaps?'

She took the cutting from the newspaper and studied it carefully before handing both items back to him.

'Why are you interested in that man in particular?'

'Because we at least know where he is and we can get him into court.'

'It all happened over forty years ago, why bring it all back?'

'For the sake of the people who were killed without mercy.'

'They're dead. They won't benefit. Who will gain, tell me that?'

'Governments will learn that people who commit crimes like these will be duly punished.'

'It hasn't stopped the atrocities by Russians in Afghanistan, Americans in Vietnam or the Khmer Rouge in Kampuchea.'

'That is soldiers against soldiers. A question of war. The women and children this man killed were innocent civilians. They had fired no shots nor committed any crimes.'

'And because of things that happened all those years ago you want me to go into a court and bring it all back.' She paused and said softly, 'And not a soul will rise from the dead.'

'You could be saving others in the future.'

She shook her head. 'It won't. And you know it. All you want is revenge.'

'You didn't answer my question.'

'What question was that?'

'Do you recognise the man in the photos?'

'I'm not going to help you.'

'You know that we can subpoena you so that you would have to come to court and answer the questions put to you about this man.'

'But you couldn't make me answer.'

'Then you would be in contempt of court.'

'And then?'

'And then the court could decide to send you to prison until you answered the questions.'

'The Germans put me in an extermination camp and you people put me in prison.' He saw the anger on her face and she screamed, 'You're all the same. You want to kill me.'

The man stood up slowly. 'I didn't come here to worry you, Mrs Cash. I'm very sorry that you're upset. Perhaps you'll think it over. Here's my card if you want to get in touch with me.'

She brushed the card aside and he put it on the mantelpiece beside the clock and then let himself out of the house.

The next morning she received a packet of photographs in the post. Photographs of trenches piled high with pitiful skeleton corpses, a small boy holding his mother's hand as they stood with SS guards alongside the queue as they waited their turn in the gas-chambers. She lit a fire in the kitchen grate and burned them, pounding the ashes to dust with a poker. An hour later she telephoned the number on the man's card and agreed to see him the next day.

He brought with him the young woman who had done the investigations with her neighbours. The woman had sounded hysterical on the telephone and he thought another woman could keep things calm.

She had made them tea and put out a plate of biscuits but her hands trembled violently as she handed them round. When she sat down she closed her eyes and said softly, 'If I talk with you, is there some way I don't have to go to court?'

The girl stopped the man from speaking and said, 'I'd like to talk to Mrs Cash alone, sir. Could you leave us for a little while?'

The man hesitated and then, obviously reluctantly, he left the room.

The young woman turned and said softly, 'Tell me what's worrying you? Why are you so scared?'

'You'll tell him, won't you?'

'Not if you don't want me to.'

'Is that a promise?'

'Yes.'

She held out her hand and drew back the sleeve to show the young woman the tattooed number on her wrist.

'Put your hand on my number and say you promise.'

The young woman touched the tattoo with her fingers. 'I promise.' She paused. 'Tell me what it's all about.'

'If I go into a court I have to swear to tell the truth. I do recognise the man. He was an SS doctor and he carried out terrible experiments on women prisoners.'

'Go on.'

'My mother's name was on the list for experiments and I begged them to cross her name off. He sent for me that night and said if I . . . slept with him . . . he'd take her name off the list.'

'How old were you then?'

'Fifteen.'

'And you slept with him?'

'Yes. But it's not that simple. He was very good to me. Gave us medicines and food and kept us off the gas-chamber rotas. I'd have to say that he saved our lives.'

'There's more than that, isn't there?'

She sighed. 'Yes.'

82

'Tell me.'

'It's my husband. He is terribly jealous of other men. He would go mad if he knew I'd been with another man. He'd count it as deceit that I hadn't told him.'

'Why didn't you tell him? After all, you were forced to do what you did.'

'I pretended to myself that it had never happened. I wanted to be married to Albert.'

'And you've both been happy ever since.'

'Yes. Very happy.'

'So you've got two worries. First of all your husband and second that your evidence would really be *for* the man, not against him. Yes?'

'Yes.'

'I don't think a court would accept evidence from an anonymous witness.'

'The court could have my name and not give it out.'

'I don't know enough about the law to comment.'

'Why not just tell your boss that I'll be a bad witness?'

'I doubt if he'd take my word for that.'

'Why don't they just forget about me? My evidence isn't going to do their case any good.'

'You can positively identify him and that's important.'

'But only you know that. I don't have to tell your boss that.'

'You'd lie to him?'

'If he insists on harassing me – yes.'

'Look. Let me talk to him and see what I can do. Meantime, stop worrying about it. Nothing may come of it. A lot of cases never get to court.'

'What is the man doing now?'

'Busch, you mean? The SS doctor?'

'Yes.'

'He bribed his way over here not long after the war. Got false papers. He worked as a salesman for one of the big drug firms. He got British citizenship about fifteen years ago. He's retired now. Lives on a small pension.'

'Is he married?'

'No. He never married.'

'Does he know your people are after him?'

'Yes. He's dead scared. It's been in the papers. The Poles wanted him to be extradited but he's a Brit now and there's no extradition treaty with the Poles. So he can only be tried over here.'

83

'But he must have applied for citizenship with his original documents and they were false. He could be deported.'

'The Brits wouldn't bother. There's dozens like him who slipped through the net.'

The buff envelope arrived a week later by registered post. It was a printed *Subpoena ad Verificandum* issued by a judge in Chambers requiring her to attend a hearing in the High Court at a date in the future which would be given her in due course. It gave both her married and unmarried names.

She leaned back against the wall of the narrow hallway and closed her eyes. She had believed that the promise would be kept and this was an unexpected blow. She was stupid to have trusted them. They didn't care that the conviction of an eighty-year-old ex-SS man would mean the end of her marriage. The end of a quiet, peaceful relationship that passing time had made seem permanent and like a rock in a strong sea. Sometimes, after one of her nightmares, she had envied the ones who had died in the camp. It was never the hunger or the pain of beatings, it was the fact that men could do such things to helpless, defenceless people. Many of them had wives and children of their own but they could still send innocent women and children to the gas chambers. Still club a defenceless man to death. Still watch the living skeletons die of starvation while they guzzled their food in the guards' canteen. And after the war she had realised that it was only an extreme version of life outside where people were equally indifferent to their neighbours' fates. And Albert, who knew nothing of such things, had been like a cave in which she could hide. She had been a fool to imagine that it could go on for ever. That she could escape from what life was all about. Violence, revenge, greed and selfishness. Every man for himself.

By the end of the day she knew what she had to do. And she knew that there wasn't much time left.

They had had their evening meal and were sitting in the parlour with the windows wide open, a breeze lifting the net curtains.

'Do you remember that boarding-house in Hastings where we went for our honeymoon?'

Albert smiled. 'Mrs Barnett or Burton, and I made the mistake that first night of saying I liked her Irish stew and we got it for three days.'

'Why don't we go there again for a couple of days?'

'Why not? We've got four hundred pounds in the building

society. We could use a bit of that.' He looked across at her affectionately. 'When do you want to go?'

'This weekend.'

'Why not? It's almost the end of the season. There'll be plenty of vacancies. I'll get the tickets tomorrow. You pack us a bag. Go Friday night, come back early on Monday.'

Albert had never seen her so full of energy. They had gone on bus rides to a dozen nearby villages. Clambered up the Downs and tramped through the woods where the leaves were beginning to turn to their autumn colours. She had persuaded him to buy three small reference guides to wild flowers, birds and butterflies. And at night they had walked along the beaches arm in arm, listening to the sounds of the ebbing tide stirring the shingle in its wake. On the train back he had said they ought to do it more often. Perhaps for her birthday weekend in October.

There had been a piece in the *Daily Express* on the Monday morning that announced that, after several meetings between the Home Secretary and a committee investigating war-crimes, a man had been arrested and charged with serious crimes against humanity. There was a picture of a man being taken from his house and a paragraph reminding readers of the outrages committed on the inmates of Auschwitz. The piece went on to refer to the allegations that the arrested man had been an SS doctor at Auschwitz who had carried out gruesome experiments on women prisoners. She read it, folded up the paper and walked slowly upstairs to the bedroom. Her bag was already packed. Five minutes later she closed the street-door behind her and walked to the railway station.

The TVS News Editor had dealt with the main item for the evening bulletin of local news – a plane crash in Ashdown forest, then turned to the researcher for the follow-up to what had been called "The bulldozer case".

'What have you got, Sally?'

'I've talked to the police, to the medical officer, to one or two people who lived around there and I've got almost nothing.'

'Tell us what you have got.'

'The cause of death was heart failure, almost certainly brought on by stress from losing her hut and made worse by what he thinks was a mixture of chronic malnutrition and hypothermia. The only thing unexplained was what looked like an old burn scar on the inside of her left wrist.'

85

'What about the police?'

'It seems she had lived in the hut in the woods for at least five years. There had been no complaints about her or her life-style. The police only got involved when the council workmen demolished her hut. But she put up no resistance. There is no information at all on her identity and there were only clothes, cooking utensils and ten pounds cash in her belongings.'

'And the neighbours?'

'Several people had seen her around when they walked in the woods. One or two of them spoke to her but she didn't reply and just backed-off to the hut. She'd never been to the local store but one of them had seen her once in Hastings. They all thought she was some sort of drop-out.'

'What are the police doing about establishing her identity?'

'Nothing, unless some member of the public phones them. There've been no calls so far.'

The News Editor leaned back in his chair. 'We'll drop it,' he said, 'it's had a fair run.' He paused. 'What about the lead from the RSPCA about the cruelty to dogs story?'

One of the things that I've tried to put over in my novels is that whether he's KGB, CIA or MI6, the man concerned is just that – a man. KGB men have wives they love and small daughters they read fairy stories to. If you've not been in the business there is a tendency to write as if our lot all wore the white hats and the KGB the black ones. The stereotyping applied to Germans too. And to some extent still does. Germans are not all arrogant, any more than all Frenchmen have the charm of Maurice Chevalier. All SS men were not brutes, especially those in the Waffen SS. Just good, tough soldiers. But you only get to know this if you spent years tracking them down and then interrogating them. I was sometimes aware, when looking at some man on the other side of my desk, that if we had lost the war I would be sitting in his chair and he in mine. There are men who are totally evil, but most of us are rather like human versions of dolly mixtures. A bit of everything. It's best not to rush to judgment.

Woman and Home *published this story in 1988.*

THE REUNION

I've never been one for reunions. If all you have in common is the same school, or even the same war, it's a pretty tenuous connection. But Manny Meyer had gone to so much trouble to trace us all that it seemed churlish to refuse. And in a way our relationship had been rather special. We had all been members of a special intelligence team hunting down real baddies after the war. I guess our characters and temperaments were very different from one another, but our training and experience had been the same. I never knew who'd picked us as a team; on the whole, he hadn't done a bad job. But that was over forty years ago.

Manny Meyer had sent us all details of how to find his house in West Sussex. Little Dornford was on the outskirts of Midhurst and I knew from experience that when houses were called Little Something-or-other it usually meant that they were mansions set in their own grounds. And Little Dornford confirmed it. The big double wrought-iron gates were works of art and led to a gravelled drive with chestnuts and beeches lining the route to what looked like a large Georgian house. A hand-written sign and an arrow indicated the car-park alongside a row of stables.

It looked as if I was the last to arrive. There was a Granada Estate, a Saab, a Volvo and a beautiful scarlet E-type Jaguar. They made my Rover look very modest. But it looked as if we had all survived quite well. For a second or two my mind went instinctively to pairing cars with owners. As it turned out I was wrong on all except two.

I saw Manny waving to me from the corner of the house and he held out his arms, beaming as I walked towards him.

87

'Chris, it's lovely to see you. They're all round at the back having a drink. What do you fancy? You name it, we've got it.'

'A fresh orange juice, if that's possible.'

'Still the same old Chris. Come on – let's join the others.'

When we'd got through the greetings and the fencing around we all settled down in the comfortable wicker armchairs. Drinks in hand and trying not to be too obvious as we examined one another and then chatted to find out what each of us was doing now.

Manny Meyer had made a fortune with Lloyd's and also had his own insurance company specialising in insuring works of art. Eddie Bailey was senior partner in a computer software house. Jerry Parsons was manager of an important orchestra and Frank Mathews had retired but still had a stake in a successful publishing house. I was surprised how staid they all were compared to what they had been as young officers.

But at dinner that night the years seemed to melt away in reminiscence.

Manny said, 'D'you remember those frightful Guards officers who ran the admin at Winchester? All that bullshit about not looking an officer in the eye and saluting his empty chair if the Commandant wasn't in his office.'

Parsons laughed. 'The best part was that those idiots stayed at the depot all the war with no promotion, and when I went back for posting to Germany I'd got my majority and the bastards had to salute me. I loved that.'

'That must have been when the depot was up in Rotherham. That lovely old house – I can't remember the name.'

Eddie said, 'Wentworth Woodhouse. Freezing cold, but dinner accompanied by Hephzibah Menuhin on the piano.' He turned and pointed his cigar at me. 'Except for you. Sloping off to the Cutlers Hall in Sheffield to waltz around with all the little factory girls.'

Parsons chipped in. 'I can remember Chris trying to teach us some dance called the Rotherham Glide.'

'A very sociable dance too,' I insisted.

Manny said, 'Why were we all chosen to do that job?'

Mathews seemed to know the background. 'We were all German speakers. We all knew the basis of the Nazi Party and German Intelligence. 21 AG did the first list but it was somebody at 30 Corps who made the final choice.'

Eddie Bailey laughed. 'And a very good choice too.' He paused.

'Can you remember that wretched operation we did to round up that underground movement, the so-called Werewolves?'

There were murmurs all round and Manny went on, 'They weren't werewolves at all, they were Hitler youth. All the top old men who'd avoided war service and fancied themselves as heroes.'

Parsons said, 'We spent weeks – months even – on that operation and I can't even remember its code-name. Can anyone else remember it?' He looked at me. 'How about you, Chris? You were in charge.'

'I can't remember. It'll come to me.'

Mathews said, 'Was it reckoned to be a success?'

'In the end it was but, as most of you will remember, it was a shambles when we started.'

Manny said, 'It was Jerry Parsons who had the first success. D'you remember, Jerry? Germans weren't allowed to move out of their town or village. But those guys were getting around all over the British Zone and part of the American Zone. And the crafty bastards had set up a transport company that gave them a legitimate excuse to be anywhere, driving vehicles.' He laughed. 'And making good money, too.'

I said, 'I can remember we had the public toilets in Göttingen as a meeting point and about midday I got a telephone call from the Bürgermeister complaining that the locals couldn't get in the toilets for all our people milling about in there speaking terrible German.'

Frank Mathews said, 'There were rumours that those old boys had a fortune stashed away for funding their operation.'

'Well, the old D-marks were useless and all accounts at all banks could be checked. If they had a fund it must have been jewellery or paintings – something like that.'

'I'd heard that it was a fund that was being used to finance Nazis who'd slipped overseas. The Odessa types.' Jerry Parsons shrugged. 'But there again – Germans couldn't send money overseas, or receive it.'

Eddie laughed. 'There were always stories of buried treasure at the bottom of lakes, Old Masters down salt mines and bags of sovereigns or Maria Theresa dollars in old castles.'

'Some of them were true, Eddie. There was a lot of loot around in those days. It wasn't just the odd Leica.'

And then the talk wandered off on to confiscated Mercs and BMWs and finally everybody headed for bed except for Jerry

89

Parsons and me. We moved to the cosy luxury of the kitchen and a pot of tea between us.

As Jerry was pouring the tea he said, 'What do you think of them?'

'The fellas?'

'Yes.'

'They strike me as being much the same as they were when we were in the army.'

Jerry looked at me for a few moments and then smiled. 'Is that why you've not kept in touch with any of them?'

'For me they were people from the war days. Not relevant to my civilian life. I followed your career in the papers.'

'You didn't really have a close relationship with any of us in those days. Was that because you were the boss?'

'No. We had jobs to do. Specialities – expertise. That was what mattered.'

'So you didn't know about Eddie Bailey?'

'What about him?'

'Well, in the unit he forged documents for us and made keys and so on. Yes?'

'Yes. That was his job.'

'But nobody bothered to work out that that skill doesn't go away just because the war's over.'

'Go on.'

'I've appeared in court three times as a character witness for Eddie Bailey.'

'You mean he forged documents?'

'No. If he'd done that he was so good I'm sure he'd have got away with it. He made little brass things for ticket machines on the Underground. And he got caught. They were wonderful copies. Precise weight and size for a one-shilling slot in a machine. I worked it out. It cost him in working time about five pounds to make just one of those tokens.'

'So why did he do it?'

'He couldn't stop doing it. When he was doing it for you he was praised for his skill but what mattered to him was beating officialdom. A beautifully faked passport, a permit or whatever was him beating authority. He couldn't stop doing it just because he was a civilian. It wasn't for gain, that's for sure. He had a good income from his legitimate business. He was hooked on beating the opposition.'

'What happened in court?'

90

'He always pleaded guilty. I said my piece about his war record. He'd get a five quid fine and a recommendation to get psychiatric help. They were always sympathetic.'

'Why didn't he contact me?'

Jerry smiled. 'You were a good skipper, Chris. But you were never one of the boys. Eddie would have been ashamed to let you know what he'd been up to.'

'That's ridiculous.'

'It isn't. And it's not a criticism of you. It's just a fact of life. You set us a fine example but the jobs we did encouraged us to want to beat the odds.' He laughed. 'Some of us got hooked on playing games.'

'Did you?'

'No. But I'd got something to go back to. For me the war was a bloody nuisance because it got in the way of music. For some – not just our group – the war was the best thing that had happened to them. And when it ended they were lost. Everything else lacked adventure and the feeling of being part of a team. It's a terrible thing to say, but wars are a good thing for a lot of men. A bit like a university.' He smiled wryly. 'Travel broadens the mind and all that.'

'Who else got hooked?'

'Frank Mathews.'

'In what way?'

'Did you know he'd been married five times since he came out of the army?'

'No. I haven't had any contact with him.'

'You remember when we had our initial training at Matlock, they told us that everybody tells lies and it might save your life if you found out right at the start what area somebody told lies about. They may be harmless lies to make somebody seem more important or glamorous than they really were. Social lies. But maybe not. And they told us how to dig those little traps for people to fall into. The casual question when you're interrogating someone. Where you already know the answer and the guy tells you a lie.

'If you're not very careful you can carry on doing that in your private life – dig holes for your nearest and dearest. They don't go much for that.'

'What's that got to do with divorces?'

'He was the best interrogator in our group. Never played the tough guy. Just grinding away slowly, wearing them down until he got the truth. Always smiling and friendly as if it were all just a game. And in a way it was. If the guy was guilty of something or other he wasn't your worry any more. You weren't involved emotionally.

'But if it's your wife or your girl-friend then you're in a different ball-game. You're involved all right. They don't like being taken apart and you don't like what you've found out.' He shrugged. 'Makes a mess.'

'But that sounds like a reason for not marrying until you're sure.'

Jerry grinned. 'It does the first time but if you go on looking for lies or deceit you have to bear in mind that what you used to dismiss as social lies can be pretty important in a marriage. If the first marriage falls apart then you resolve not to dig pits next time round. After all, she ain't the Gestapo.

'So when the little bells ring in your head and the little red lights start flashing you ignore them and you become more gullible than the average man. So . . .' He shrugged. '. . . so you get taken for a ride – again and again.'

'So why keep getting married? Just stay single. Why doesn't the new woman look at the record?'

'Oh, she does. But Frank's a very attractive fellow. They fall for him and he's off. Searching for the one who'll make it all come true. I think the present one will do the trick but only time will tell.'

'And you blame this on his job with me?'

'No. The war and the job just gave him the weapons. Nobody realised that there was a self-destruct button built-in.'

'Anything else I should know?'

Parsons laughed. 'I'd say that's enough. Maybe I shouldn't have said anything but I thought maybe you ought to know.'

'Why?'

'Why should you know?'

'Yes.'

'I heard talk that you still had connections at MI6. Even that you were still with them.'

'And if I was, why should I know these things?'

'You really want to know?'

'Yes.'

'Because MI6 are still doing the things we did. Taking men and turning them into efficient agents and never thinking about what they're doing to them.'

'Like what?'

'Berlin for a week, then two days in Paris, a month in Rio and then home for a couple of days.'

'What's wrong with that?'

'When they're not on the job they're sitting in some tatty hotel room. Can't ring home – if they've got a home – because it's against the rules. They're supposed to be Foreign Office. So what do they do? They go out and drink too much or screw some hooker. Or both.' He paused and looked at me. 'The wages of sin ain't death – it's being desperately unhappy and lonely.'

'But you've survived and Manny has too.'

'Manny. Manny never went along with all the training stuff. Manny looked after himself from day one. Not that I blame him.'

'Most people did, to one degree or another.'

Parsons laughed. 'Not like our Manny. Manny always had one eye on the main chance. It was his antidote to being a hero. A kind of insurance policy.'

'I don't understand.'

'There's no need to, Chris. Maybe I've said too much.'

'What kind of insurance do you mean?'

For a moment Parsons hesitated and then he said quietly, 'Think about what we talked about this evening. That thing against the so-called Werewolves.' He stood up as I opened my mouth to speak. 'No. No more. Just think it all over.'

In bed that night I read for ten minutes and then switched off the bedside light. I thought about what Parsons had told me. It was a fairly shrewd analysis even when it came to me. Two marriages up the spout but not for the reasons he gave; and sometimes looking out of a hotel window in a strange city, wondering if this was how I really wanted to spend my life. But come the bright morning, I knew it was what I chose to do. I could have retired a couple of years back but I liked the job. Knowing what was going on behind the scenes, knowing what was going to happen long before it happened.

We'd known about Eddie Bailey's court appearances and we'd put a word in the appropriate ear. Eddie was a genuine victim but Frank Mathews was different. He should never have been used as a field-officer. An excellent interrogator but not an action man. But in the war and immediately after you had to use the bodies you'd got. He was a clever, nice, but essentially weak man.

But I wondered what the hints about Manny Meyer amounted to. Anyway, it was all a long time ago.

The next morning Manny had shown us round the mansion, beaming with amiable pleasure as we all admired his house. Manny's wife was on holiday in Israel but Manny was being looked after by several servants.

We had an early snack and then said our goodbyes, vowing to keep contact now it had finally been made, knowing full well that, like friendships made on a cruise, the best we should do was a Christmas card if we remembered.

It had taken Archives a week to get me the old files on the Werewolf operation in 1946. There were two covering the detailed plan and its execution and a file containing only the interrogation reports of the Nazis who had been arrested.

I read the interrogation reports through twice. There were only twenty of them. Half a dozen of the interrogations had been done by me and the arrest reports were signed by me. It seemed odd to be reading them after all those years. Typed by Sergeant McKay on the old Olivetti Lettera. But there was nothing significant about Manny Meyer. His name was on a couple of arrest reports but he hadn't done the interrogations. I was going to send them back, but for no particular reason I decided to hang on to them for another day.

It was on the Sunday night that the penny dropped and I took a taxi to Century House and went up to my office. It was the interrogation of Hoffman that I wanted to check again. It was one of mine. He was their admin man and I'd asked him how they were financing the transport operation. He'd said it paid for itself but I knew he was lying. The transport business was just a means for them to go wherever they wanted in Germany. Their permits to operate were forgeries and there was no way they could have broken even, let alone formed a terrorist organisation. They had been responsible for the deaths of a few British troops. Oil on the roads that could turn over an army truck and wires across roads that would decapitate motorcycle dispatch riders.

So I kept the pressure on Hoffman about their funds. It was illegal to transfer money from one bank to another so it couldn't be actual cash. Gold had to be declared so that was dangerous. But despite threats and offers of deals, Hoffman wouldn't talk. It was odd because I sensed that he was ready to talk but was scared. And as far as I could see, there was nothing more to be scared of now. He was in the bag already.

Just on a hunch I phoned down for Manny's "P" file. It was thicker than I expected. His name was on the file cover – Louis Emanuel Meyer. But most of it was press cuttings. Manny was a very rich man who had gone from small beginnings to complicated company takeovers until he was the major shareholder in a huge conglomerate. Most of the cuttings were from the *Financial Times* and the financial pages of other papers. There were clippings of his wedding and photographs of him and his wife, Leah.

Then there was a two-page spread from a women's magazine. There was a photograph of Manny and Leah and a black labrador. The article touched briefly on his East End youth and his service in the army and then went on to paint a picture of the man himself – his life-style and his interests away from business affairs. This led to a joking reference to his golf handicap and the success of the string of racehorses that he owned. And there it was. The girl interviewer asked him about his hobby of philately. Experts had said that he had the finest collection of German stamps outside Germany itself. He had fenced the question by talking of his collection of Penny Blacks, but my mind went back to when he was showing us around the mansion. The library and its separate shelves of beautiful leather-bound stamp albums. There must have been forty of them and more than half had "*Deutschland*" gilded on their spines. The interviewer had gone on to quote a figure from a philatelic magazine valuing Manny's German collection alone at £500,000. Ingenious thinking on the part of the German terrorists and typical reaction from Manny Meyer.

Just like Jerry Parsons had said – Manny was always on the look-out for personal insurance. But I wondered why Parsons had given me the hint so long after the event. Whatever the reason, I didn't want to know. Like I said – I was never one for reunions.

Like the fictional character in the story I'm not fond of reunions whether they are school, rugby club or service reunions. But I did go to one or two and in real life I was in fact slightly taken aback by how respectable my chaps were in Civvy Street. Bank managers and civil servants who had once been rather gung-ho were to a man proud fathers and upright citizens. I was the only one not wearing a three-piece suit.

THE ROCKING-HORSE SPY

As he sat on the bench in the Science Museum watching Robbie turn the handle of one of the glass-cased models, he wondered why his day with his son never seemed to come up to his expectations. The place was full of men like him – divorced fathers with "access" on alternate Saturdays. There was no chance of being a real father. If he asked questions about what the boy did at home it was called "snooping", trying to find out what she was up to. And there was just a very faint element of truth in the accusation. But if you couldn't be a real father, what could you be? A pal? What eight-year-old boy wants a forty-year-old pal? He thought about him so much when he wasn't with him but, somehow, it never seemed possible to express his feelings to the boy when they were together. Access Saturdays had become a grim, arid desert of frustration and disappointment. But the small boy seemed to take it in his stride.

Patterson smiled to himself as he watched his son, one stocking down to his ankle, his face intent on the wheels of the model turning slowly. A small girl walked up and stood watching with a man who was obviously her father. There was a second handle to the model, that worked a crane, and the girl reached out to turn it. Then to his dismay his son roughly pushed aside the little girl. 'Go away,' he shouted. 'This is mine.'

He hurried over. 'Apologise at once, Robbie. Say you're sorry.'

'I'm not sorry. This is my model.'

'Say you're sorry or we shall leave right away.'

The man with the small girl smiled diffidently. 'It's OK. It doesn't matter.'

Patterson caught his son's arm, swinging him round to face the girl.

'Say it. Say you're sorry.'

For a moment there was defiance then Robbie said reluctantly, 'I'm sorry.'

Patterson turned to the man. 'I'm sorry he was rude to your little girl.' He smiled. 'This is his favourite model but that's no excuse.'

The man smiled. 'I understand.' He shrugged. 'They are just children.'

'How about we all go to the café upstairs and have an ice-cream?'

'It's not necessary – really.'

'I'd like to.'

The man shrugged and smiled. 'OK. Let's do that.'

As they sipped their coffees Patterson looked at the girl's father. His clothes were old-fashioned and his thin woollen tie had an untidy knot at his throat. His face was out of some Dickens novel. Large spaniel eyes, a full mouth; it was the face of a sad comedian.

When the children had eaten their ice-creams and were playing a guessing game, the two men were having a second coffee and Patterson said, 'Are you an "access father"?'

The man frowned. 'I don't understand. What is an "access father"?'

When Patterson had explained the other man said, 'My wife was killed in a car accident six months ago. But, like you, I think I am a poor father.' He smiled diffidently. 'Plenty of love but no practical experience.'

'You speak very good English but you've got a slight accent.'

The man smiled. 'Part French, part Russian.'

'Have you lived here long?'

'Nearly a year now. I'm a freelance journalist. I write about electronics and computers.'

'Who do you write for?'

'Magazines, newspapers.' He smiled. 'Anyone who'll take my stuff.'

'Is that why you come to the Science Museum?'

The man laughed. 'No. We generally go to the Natural History Museum but it's closed today for building work.'

'Have you been to the zoo yet?'

'No.'

'How about we take the children to the zoo in two weeks' time? That's when I have Robbie again.'

'Why not? Where shall we meet?'

'Let's meet at the main entrance to the zoo at one o'clock.'

'Fine. I'll look forward to that.'

There was a message for him at the security desk. He was to go immediately to Logan's office.

He was surprised when he saw that it was not only Logan but also Chester and Harris who were waiting for him.

Logan pointed to a spare chair. 'Sit down, Patterson.'

When he was seated Logan leaned forward, his elbows on his desk. 'Where were you on Saturday?'

Patterson looked surprised. 'I had my son for the day.'

'Where did you go?'

'We had a snack at a hamburger place in Kensington. We went to a museum and then I took Robbie home.'

'Which museum was it?'

'The Science Museum.'

'Why did you go to that particular place?'

Patterson shrugged. 'What the hell is all this?'

'Why did you go there?'

'We go there frequently. My boy likes it there.'

'Tell us about Malik.'

'Who the hell is Malik?'

'You talked with him for nearly an hour in the museum café.'

Patterson explained what had happened and Logan said, 'What did you talk about?'

'His daughter and my son.' He shrugged. 'Just social chit-chat.'

'Didn't his name ring a bell?'

'I didn't ask his name. Why should I?'

'His name's Malik.'

'So what?'

'He's a Russian. Suspected KGB.'

'He told me he was a technical journalist.'

'He is. That's his cover. What else did he tell you?'

'Nothing. But we're taking our kids to the zoo in a couple of weeks' time.'

'Who suggested that?'

'I did.'

'Why?'

For the first time in the interview Patterson felt a surge of anger but he said quietly, 'Because it's very difficult, and rather lonely, trying to entertain a small child for a day and doing it as a foursome with someone with the same problem makes it easier.'

'Was that the only reason?'

'For God's sake. What other reason could there be?'

Before Logan could reply, Chester intervened. Chester was the senior of the three of them.

'What were your impressions of the Russian, Mr Patterson?' Chester spoke quietly and calmly and looked as if he would value Patterson's opinion.

'He seemed a quiet sort of man. Polite. Spoke excellent English. Obviously loved his little girl.'

'Did you like him? Did you feel you could get on with him on a friendly basis?'

'I didn't think about him that way. He was just a casual acquaintance.'

'I think your meeting could be very helpful.' Chester turned to look at Logan. 'I'd like to suggest that Mr Patterson takes over the surveillance of our friend Malik. He's in an ideal position to keep a close eye on him.'

Logan obviously resented the interference of his senior but agreed without protest to the new arrangement.

Patterson sat in his own office and read the details on Malik's file. He was forty-two. Born in Moscow. Languages at Moscow University and a science degree at Leningrad. Had served for six years at their embassy in Washington. Wife died in car collision in Kiev. One child. Father Russian. Mother French. There was little else beyond the surveillance reports.

The reports showed that he had contacted a wide span of high-technology industries in the UK and France. But it was no more than any conscientious science writer would have done. But equally, they were exactly the targets that a KGB man briefed to get secret technological information would have aimed at. A casual observer would never have seen Malik as an enemy agent but Patterson had been in MI5 too long to go by appearances. They didn't have to have their eyes close together or horns growing out of their foreheads. All too often they looked like your Uncle Charlie. And after all they probably *were* somebody's Uncle Charlie. Or Ivan, or Igor. Or in Malik's case, Grigor.

*

It was a fine day for the visit to the zoo and the children got on well together. Malik and Patterson sat on a bench in the sunshine as the children watched the sea-lions being fed. It was Malik who seemed to want to talk.

'My name's Malik. Grigor Malik. What's yours?'

'Patterson. Joe Patterson. Joe.'

'Shall I call you Joe?'

'Of course.'

'You live in London?'

'Yes. In Chelsea. A couple of rooms. And you?'

'I live in Chiswick.' He smiled. 'I've got a girl-friend. If things work out, maybe we get married. Maria likes her very much. It's her small house where we live. She's very kind to us both.' He nodded as he smiled. 'I like her very much.' He paused. 'I'd like you to meet her.'

'I'd like that, Grigor.'

'We could go back there for tea today. I told her I might bring you and the boy back, if you agreed.'

'Fine. I'd enjoy that.'

'Do you have a new girl?'

'A few girl-friends but nothing serious.'

'You're not lonely, living alone?'

'Sometimes. But I get by.'

'How long have you been divorced?'

'Two years.'

'Is she married again?'

'Yes.'

The small terraced house in Chiswick was neat and well-kept. More or less what he had expected. But the girl-friend Kathie was a surprise. Irish, very pretty, lively and in her mid-twenties. And she obviously adored Malik and his daughter.

The children were playing in Maria's bedroom and the three of them sat around talking. Music and books.

She laughed, putting her hand on Malik's arm as she looked at Patterson. 'This one's a romantic. So it's Russian music and French novels. Proust and Flaubert with Rachmaninov and Tchaikovsky in the background.' She turned to look at Malik. 'Did you tell Joe about the rocking-horse?'

Malik smiled. 'No. You tell him.'

Kathie smiled. 'He's seen one of those beautifully carved rocking-horses and he's tempted to buy it for Maria. Do you

101

know how much they cost? Three hundred pounds. It's crazy. He's going to borrow it from a bank.' She smiled at Malik affectionately. 'He's a big softy, this man.'

Malik smiled. 'That's what fathers are for, my love.'

The rocking-horse had been bought and the little girl's delight was obviously well-rewarding to Malik.

All through the summer Patterson had been a regular visitor to the house in Chiswick. Sometimes with Robbie and sometimes alone. In the early days he had found it disturbing to have such a close relationship with a man he was investigating. But as time went on and he was convinced that Malik was what he claimed to be – a journalist – he relaxed. He was aware that Malik had never revealed his nationality but there was no occasion when it would have been particularly appropriate. Robbie enjoyed his time with Maria and the Chiswick house had become almost a second home for both of them.

Patterson found it irksome when Logan congratulated him on his achieving such a close and useful relationship with a suspect. It made him aware of his own duplicity both to Logan and to Malik.

He had had long talks with the people who Malik had talked to at the various high-tech companies. There was no doubt that he was persuading people to give him information far beyond what was needed for genuine technical articles. And in some cases Malik had pretended to be a French national. But subterfuge and even deceit were not unknown to ordinary journalists. And he suggested this when submitting his reports to Logan. But Logan didn't share his views. For him Malik was a spy, an industrial spy maybe, but a spy all the same. Industrial espionage was part of the KGB's function in the West. They saved the Soviet Union billions of roubles in research costs, stealing from the NATO allies just as purposefully as they tried to undermine the fabric of western society.

Because of his views on Malik he was not consulted on the department's evaluation of his reports. He was shocked when he saw the piece on the front page of the *Evening Standard* which said that three suspect Russians were being held on suspicion of spying. There were grainy pictures of all of them and one was of Malik. The *Daily Mail* the next day reported that the three Russians were being expelled.

In his time in MI5 he had been responsible for the prosecution and imprisonment of many people but they had been virtual strangers.

Objects of suspicion, people to be kept under surveillance from a distance. He knew little about the effect of his work on their lives. And he had always been convinced of their guilt. But Malik was different. When he talked to Logan about his doubts, it was obvious that he wasn't interested. The Russians had thrown out two diplomats from the British Embassy in Moscow and London wanted to retaliate. They didn't necessarily have to be guilty of anything substantial. Malik was just an easy and available victim.

Some instinct made him want to see the girl, Kathie, and on the second day he'd gone out to Chiswick and walked to the road of old-fashioned Victorian houses. As he approached number sixteen he saw a small group of people and then he saw the "For Sale" notice.

He made his way through the people to the front door. It was open and there was a handwritten notice saying that the sale of goods was on the following day. He walked into the front room. There were rows of domestic bits and pieces each marked with a price. Kettles, a toaster, a box of cutlery, crockery, plants in pots, a radio and TV and a record-player. Rolled up rugs and carpets, small items of furniture. And on a table by the far wall was the rocking-horse. He looked at the card pasted to the leather saddle. It said: "Not for sale. Deliver to Gt. Ormond St. Children's Hospital". As he turned away she was standing at the door looking at him. Her eyes red from weeping.

She said, 'They told me I could put up the prices because they were souvenirs of a spy.'

'But these are your things, Kathie, and why are you selling the house?'

'Was it you?'

'Was what me?'

'Somebody must have been watching him. They let me see him in the police cell for ten minutes. He said they knew everything about him. Me . . .' She shrugged helplessly.

'Did he say that he thought it was me?'

'No. He said you were his only friend.' She paused. 'They don't care about people, do they?'

'Did you know he was spying?'

She laughed harshly. 'If he was a spy then you and I are spies. What lies they all tell.'

'If there's anything I can do to help you, will you let me know?'

'You mean you can find me a nice, gentle man who loves me, and spends all his savings on a rocking-horse for a small girl?'

'I'll call in next week.'

'I won't be here.'

'Where will you be?'

'I've no idea. But I won't be here.' And he saw the tears on her cheeks as he turned to leave.

The Russians were on *News at Ten* that night. At Heathrow. Photographers and reporters running alongside them. As they stopped at the air-side gate a reporter thrust a microphone up to the first Russian. 'Have you got any comment, Mr Kreski?' The big, sour-faced Russian said, 'This country stinks.' A girl reporter spoke to Malik. He was carrying one case and Maria. The little girl was white faced, one arm around her father's neck. 'How do you feel about being expelled, Mr Malik?' For a moment Malik was silent and then he said, 'I am very sad to be leaving. I had good friends here. We liked it here, my daughter and I. People were very . . .'

Patterson leaned forward and switched off the TV.

Until recently the public in the West has had its vision of Russians based on those po-faced comrades lining the Kremlin walls while the rockets and tanks roll by in Red Square. This is not due to crafty propaganda by the West but because we never had a chance to see ordinary Russians. This can lead to a lot of misconceptions. I can still remember a friend who had been on one of those five-day package trips to Moscow describing with vivid detail and much moulding with the hands this fantastic blonde he had seen in Moscow. Why should he be so amazed that out of a population of 300 million there might be a beautiful girl or two? The simple explanation is that Soviet newsreels and films gave the impression that good Soviet ladies were all spending their time repairing the roads in Moscow and were built like the proverbial brick out-houses. Tchaikovsky, Rachmaninov and Glazunov must be turning in their graves. This short story was meant to show that most

Russian men are not like those on the Kremlin wall but much like the rest of us.

"The Rocking-horse Spy" *was first published by* Woman's Own *in 1986 and was reprinted in the* South China Morning Post *in 1987.*

YOU WERE NEVER LOVELIER

———

Judge Abrahams had one of those faces that journalists inevitably describe as weather-beaten. The tan certainly came from golf played in all weathers, but the sad brown eyes were the products of his genes and many years of listening to the foolishness, ruthlessness and greed of the men and women who stood in the dock before him. He had already announced his retirement next year. Fifteen years presiding over cases at the Central Criminal Court was, in his opinion, enough for any man. He would be seventy-three on his next birthday and he had grown tired of the conflict between the law and his politics. Those rosy student days of the *New Statesman* and the Left Book Club and the belief that at last there was an answer to humanity's problems. And then the slow realisation, as his career in the law progressed, that none of it, neither socialism nor Christianity, would work. And it was people, just ordinary human beings, that made them unworkable.

He looked at his watch. He'd adjourned the court until 2 p.m. Another five minutes. And as he pushed aside his glass of wine, his thoughts went to the woman. She was the epitome of all the lost dreams, all the hopes of the old days. And of all the conflicts he had had in his mind since the war had ended. The sentence he would pass was the result of her deliberate defiance of society and the law. He had no choice. The letter and the spirit of the law required it. But she didn't deserve it. If ever there was a case of visiting the sins of the fathers on their children, this was it. It was Colby who ought to be in the dock. Smooth, charming Colby. Ex-MI6, and now supposedly an officer in the KGB, pontificating on the ineptitude of his former colleagues while still trying to play

107

the English gentleman. Cricket on the village green and all that. But still the shifty eyes and the crooked grin.

He pressed the usher's bell and put on his robe and wig in front of the long mirror.

Judge Abrahams looked at the woman as the wardress forced her to stand up in the box. Pale face, wispy fair hair, her face just a faint echo of what must have been attractive features when she was a girl. But enough of that.

'Mary Lewis, I have listened carefully to what has been said in your defence by your Counsel. And let me say that I accept that the discovery that you are the illegitimate daughter of Mark Colby, a traitor and a spy, is something that has caused you great concern.

'The revelation may well have played a part in your antisocial and criminal behaviour over the years. I accept too that it has probably affected you throughout your life.

'However, the crime of blackmail is a particularly reprehensible one and when I look at your past convictions – a dozen convictions for dishonesty – you leave me no choice but to sentence you as the law requires me to.' He paused. 'Have you anything you wish to say?'

She turned and spat at the policewoman beside her then turned to the judge, pointing her finger at him as she screamed, 'You fascist pig!' And then the policewoman bundled her down the steps to the cells.

An elderly woman sat alone in the public gallery until the next case started and then left, walking unsteadily with the aid of a stick. In the corridor she dabbed her eyes with a cambric handkerchief, looking into the distance as if she was gathering strength for the walk to the top of the main steps. She had seen the paragraph in the *Evening Standard* and the two names – Mark Colby and Mary Lewis – had leaped out from the page. It had just given the date of the hearing and the barest details of the charges. She had had to come.

When she got home John had already laid the table for their evening meal. The french windows were open and she could see him in the garden, sitting in the deckchair, his eyes closed. They had never really loved each other. Not even in the beginning. But they had needed one another and had done so ever since. It had seemed enough in those far-off days. He still worked for the bank. Still pleasant looking. Still amiable. But without a spark of imagination. His favourite expression had always been "You've got to take things as you find them."

He saw her, waved to her and got up from the deckchair and came into the house.

'You're back early. I didn't expect you back until after eight.'

'It was a bit cold.'

'There's always a breeze off the sea at Southend this time of year.' He smiled. 'You go on the pier?'

'Yes. But most of the things were closed.'

'Ah well, at least you had a breath of sea air.'

For a fleeting moment she wondered what he would say if she told him what she'd really been doing. Three days of lying. She consoled herself that it was as much for his benefit as hers.

In bed that night she lay awake, alone. There were people laughing and singing in the street below. Not rowdily. Just happy as they went on their way.

He had loved parties, had Mark. He'd come into her small office that day. All that charm and that funny smile. Said he was going to a party that evening and didn't want to go alone. How about she came with him? He looked like a little boy lost. All alone.

But in fact he'd been the centre of attraction. The one who played the piano. Smiling at her through the press of people. She remembered the words that he sang as he looked at her, smiling affectionately: 'You were never lovelier . . .'

There had been lots more parties and she had hated them. All those ghastly queers. Ignoring her. Joking with him as if they shared some secret. Quoting Latin tags, roaring with laughter at nothing. And then the wildness. The bottle smashing, the vomiting. They thought they were so superior and that behaving like hooligans was their special privilege.

Mark had laughed at her criticisms and said she was a prude. But he'd kissed her and they'd gone to a friend's flat for the night. It was never to his place even though his wife lived out of London in the country. And she shared her room with Paula. And Paula detested him. Said the charm was phoney. Just one more married man having an affair.

When she'd gone to the doctor it was because she thought she had a stomach ulcer. She had been horrified when he told her that she was pregnant.

Mark had been cold and indifferent when she told him. Said

she was a stupid little bitch not to take any precautions. When she had asked him what she should do he'd shrugged and said it was up to her. He was posted abroad and for four weeks she had been demented with worry. Her parents would have been horrified if she told them. Even Paula showed no sympathy. But Paula had got her the address and lent her the money. For the last three months of the pregnancy she had lived in a boarding-house in St Albans. She had signed away her rights to the baby a week before it was born.

In the cell at Holloway Prison two wardresses were trying to restrain the frantic, violent woman whose voice was hoarse with shouting. She had torn to shreds the prison uniform and ripped the mattress on the wooden bed so that its coarse horsehair stuffing covered the stone floor of the cell.

Eventually the prisoner was exhausted, sitting on the edge of the bed, her head in her hands, rocking back and forth as she sobbed, her body shaking as if with an ague.

The two wardresses stood trying to rearrange their torn uniforms, wiping the sweat from their faces.

The older one said quietly, 'Mother of God. I'd like to get my hands on whoever brought her to this state. They should be in here with her.'

She was fifteen when Matron had sent for her. Matron was a spinster. And far removed from the usual portrayal of spinsters. She had a loving heart and a determination to see that her charges were helped in every possible way to go out into the world as little scarred by their abandonment as possible.

In the year before the law allowed them to leave if they so chose, she had the duty to tell them the facts of their origins. Nothing that needed to be said was avoided, no matter how disagreeable it might be. She believed that it was better that they learned the facts from her than by gossip or accident. They wanted to know. But it meant the end of those dreams of being the heir to some fortune or the offspring of some famous person. It meant coming down to earth and facing the terrible, simple fact that most of them had been abandoned simply because they were not wanted.

'Sit down, Mary.' When the girl was sitting she went on, 'In the year before girls leave here I have a talk with them about their origins.' She smiled. 'If I know anything, that is. In your case I'm doing it a little early for a reason that I'll explain.

110

'I had a call from a newspaper a week ago. From a woman journalist. She'd been doing some checking-up for a story. I refused to give her any information about you or even confirm that you were here. But they never give up on these things and, just in case you might hear from other people, I thought I'd better have a word with you now.' Matron glanced at a sheet of paper in front of her and then looked back at the girl.

'Have you ever heard the name Colby? Mark Colby?'

'No, Miss Flower.'

'Well, Mr Colby was a spy for the Russians. He was British, an intelligence officer who worked for the British Secret Service. And for reasons best known to him, he used his position to spy for the Russians. In the end he defected. Went to Moscow and has been there ever since. You were about two when he defected, and already with us here. Mark Colby was your father.'

For a few moments the girl was silent, then she said, 'Who was my mother?'

'Your mother was a civil servant. She was a secretary in the same organisation as your father.'

'Why didn't they want me?'

'They weren't married and your father was already married. He had other children.'

'What was she like? My mother.'

'I don't know, Mary. I never met her. You came here straight from the nursing home.'

'Are they both still alive?'

'Your father is. I don't know about your mother.'

'What was my mother's name?'

'I usually get both parents' names but in your case, probably because of your father's work, I was not given your mother's name. The only reason why I know about your father is that they had to tell me because of the unusual secrecy. And not long afterwards he went to Moscow.'

'Where was I born?'

'In St Albans.'

'Where's that?'

'It's north of London.'

'Does this mean I've got to leave the orphanage?'

'Certainly not. You have to stay here for another fourteen months. After that you can stay, if you want to, until you're twenty-one.'

'What do I do when I leave?'

'What would you like to do?'

For several moments the girl was silent and then she said, 'Maybe if I wrote to him in Moscow, he'd come and see me.'

'I shouldn't do that, Mary.'

'But he might like me. He could tell me who she is and where I could find her.'

'Think about it, child. You're doing well in school. You could have a good life. Independent. An interesting job.'

The girl smiled. 'Can I go now, Matron?'

'Yes.'

The letter had been addressed to "Mark Colby, KGB, Moscow, Russia". It had been picked up in the routine check and read, copied and passed to MI6 liaison.

An ad hoc committee of four had discussed what to do with the letter. It seemed innocent enough. It had been checked by a cryptographer for secret codes and invisible writing but both tests were negative. It came down to what benefits would accrue to the intelligence service if it were sent or not sent.

The contents seemed innocuous enough.

Dear Mr Colby,

My name is Mary. I am your daughter. I am in my last year at St Anne's Orphanage near Crowborough in Sussex. I thought you might like to know that I am OK.

I would like to hear from you. Would you like me to come and live with you in Moscow? From what I have read you sound a bit lonely. I know how you feel. I can cook quite well.

I would also like to know my mother's name. I would like to find her.

Your loving daughter,

Mary Lewis

(Was this my mother's name?)

When the security branch of the GPO police passed the letter to MI6 there was some discussion as to whether it should be allowed to make its way to Moscow. The more cynical were amused at the naivety of anyone thinking that Mark Colby could be moved by a young girl's tentative reaching out. The charm was as practical as armour plating. His heart had never been touched by the fate of his victims, be they wives, mistresses, friends or the dead victims of his betrayals. Some argued that it was selfishness rather than hardness, and others argued that they were the same thing. But there seemed no point in stopping the letter and it was put back into the normal postal system.

At the KGB's headquarters in Dzerdzhinski Square a similar discussion took place as to whether the letter should be allowed through. KGB men were trained to be suspicious. Distrust of others was in-built both by their training and experience. But there is a vast difference between distrust and cynicism. Suspicion and distrust kept wild animals alive, cynicism was confined to humans.

So the discussions were longer in Moscow. Spreading over several days and covering a wide spectrum of questions. Would Colby be upset by the contact from his daughter? Or maybe be embarrassed by it? Would it make him homesick for England? Was it perhaps some ploy by British intelligence to lure him back? The same chemical and code tests were carried out as in London. With the same negative results.

At no time was it suggested that the Englishman would be indifferent to his daughter's appeal. Russians have a natural love for children and families and the officers concerned were aware of what their own feelings would be if they were in Colby's place. Sadness, some regrets, some guilt.

It was decided to pass the letter on and offer help if it was necessary. Volkov was ordered to hand the letter over personally. He reported back that Colby had read the letter, then screwed it up and thrown it in the wastepaper basket and carried on talking about his views on training agents for work in the United States.

During the next six months there had been more letters from the girl, obviously distressed that she was getting no response. Colby had indicated to Volkov that he wasn't interested, the letters should be destroyed. There were mixed feelings in Dzerdzhinski Square about Colby's attitude. Some saw it as a sign of great inner strength and commitment to the Soviet Union, but others found it unnatural and heartless. Volkov, who had three children, found Colby's attitude incomprehensible. What would it cost to send a few lines of comfort to the girl? Maybe next time he was in London himself he'd do something about it.

John had gone to his chess club meeting that night but she still felt guilty as she pressed the button for BBC1 and settled back in her chair. As the *Panorama* titles came up, she wondered if it wouldn't be better to turn over to something else. But even as she thought about it there was the picture of Red Square and St Basil's. She reached for her knitting as if its familiarity might protect her.

There was a close-up of the face of the journalist who was going to interview him. Going over the same old stuff again about spies and double-agents, the war and how it all happened.

Then they were in his flat. Shelves of books behind him. He looked very old in the brown cardigan. There were bags under his eyes. He'd always had bags under his eyes but they were worse now because of the sunken cheeks. He was bent forward in his chair with an old man's stoop. But his eyes were the same, with that same old look as if he was terribly interested in what the interviewer was saying. He did that automatically to everybody. He'd laughed when she had told him and he'd said it made people feel important. As if what they said really mattered. It always amazed her that people were taken in by it. And there he was, still using that little boy look. The misunderstood man.

'And I understand you still phone London for the Test Match scores? Do you miss England?'

He smiled amiably. 'I'm afraid not. This is my home. This is my country. Always has been.'

'And now you're married to a Russian lady?'

The deprecating shrug and smile. 'She's wonderful. Just what I always wanted.'

'What was it you wanted?'

'Somebody whom I could trust completely. Somebody who was honest and straightforward. Somebody I could rely on. Somebody who cared about me.' He nodded his head as if he agreed with what he was saying.

'Do you still have contacts in England?'

'Of course. I correspond with many of my old friends, people I care about. The people who were important to me in the old days.'

'No regrets about those old days?'

'No. None whatever.'

'No regret for the damage you did? The lives you lost?'

'In a war people get hurt. It's very sad, but it happens.'

'What about friends of those days who felt you betrayed them?'

'Apart from politics and the war, I never betrayed a soul.' He paused and looked at the interviewer, the camera in close-up on his face. 'I care too much about people to deceive or betray. That's why I'm here in Moscow. Nobody suffered in any relationship with me. Perhaps if I had been more – what shall I say? – selfish, things would have gone better for me. I cared about people. I still do.'

'And now you're an officer in the KGB and . . .'

She switched off angrily, her heart beating so fast that she could hardly breathe.

She could never understand why they always let him get away with such a pack of lies. He had had spells of being a journalist and maybe it was that. There was a phrase she'd heard him say: "Dog don't eat dog". Maybe that was it. He only had to lift a finger and they all came running, eager to interview him. But none of them asked about the men who had died because of him, the cavalier seduction of the wives of friends and colleagues; and those cold blue eyes weren't twinkling when he had told her she was on her own. She could still remember the words after all those years.

'What the hell did you expect me to say?'

'I don't know. I thought maybe you'd tell me what to do.'

'About what?'

'About having the baby – or not.'

'What do you want to do?'

'It depends on what you want.'

He shrugged his shoulders. 'Don't bother about me.'

'I thought you might want me to have the baby.' She had meant to say 'our baby' but she lost her nerve.

'Why on earth do you think that?'

'I don't know.' She shook her head and shrugged. 'Will you be angry if I have it?'

'I'll be in Washington, Mary. I'm leaving in a couple of days' time.'

'How long will you be there?'

'Who knows? It's an established posting. At least a couple of years.'

'I'll miss you, Mark.'

'Don't take it all so seriously.' He smiled. 'How about I take you out to dinner tonight and then we'll go to Roger's place? He's having one of his parties before he goes to Cairo.'

'No, thanks. The less I see of that ghastly man, the better.'

He laughed. 'Most women like queers because they're charming and no danger.'

'I wouldn't like Roger even if he wasn't a queer.'

'Why not?'

'He's an arrogant, disgusting man and a drunk. He thinks he's still at Oxford.'

'It was Cambridge.' He smiled. 'Anyway, I'll see you again before I go.'

He hadn't seen her again. But she had seen him. She'd stood in the shadows across the street from Roger Borthwick's flat. She'd heard him playing the piano until it was drowned by the shouting and the blare of a radio or a gramophone. It was 2 a.m. when he came out with two other men. The three of them laughing as they waved drunkenly to passing taxis. Some of which slowed down and then drove on. One of the three was vomiting over the rails of a basement.

She had screwed up her courage to ask him if he'd lend her the money either to have an abortion or to go into hospital and have the baby. But she knew when she saw him that night that she really was on her own. She and her problems were already forgotten.

It had been 1944 and her parents would have been horrified if they knew she had slept with a man, let alone a married man. And to know that she was pregnant would have been more than they could cope with.

In the end she sat in her small bed-sitter one night and made a list of the pros and cons between having an abortion and having a baby. There was no doubt where the balance lay. Having an abortion would wipe the slate clean. There were few pros for having the baby.

Making out the list had helped her make up her mind. Despite the list she decided to have the baby and then have it taken care of by one of the societies that did that sort of thing.

She had given a month's notice at work when she was five months pregnant but nobody seemed to have noticed her condition. But in the week before she left, two men had come to her office from some other part of Broadway House and asked her about Mark Colby. They had been relaxed and easy-going and she had wondered why they were so interested in him. But if you worked for MI6 you were used to the way they did things. They were halfway through the interview when she realised that, although they didn't actually say so, they knew she was pregnant. And who the father was. The older man had asked if she needed any help with anything but, when she shook her head, he let it pass. They asked about who his friends were. How often he stayed at the office after normal hours. They checked the copying machine chits and told her that they were removing the filing cabinets to some other part of the building. Just routine, they said, because he was now overseas. They asked if she had a passport and seemed pleased that she didn't have one. And that was it. They'd smiled, thanked her for her help and told her to forget that they'd talked with her. It was just routine. But she'd worked for MI6 for three years and she knew better than that.

She never saw the baby. It seemed that was part of the strict procedure. She'd given a false name – Lewis, after an aunt she liked, and they'd let her name the baby and she'd said it should be Mary.

She got herself a job as secretary to a bank manager and moved into a two-roomed flat in Croydon, not far from her parents in Purley. She had had vague hopes of doing something more interesting but she didn't know what. And in the end it had all fizzled out. She had met John at the bank. He had come from Head Office to do an audit. He had a flat somewhere in Finchley. She had never been to it and he'd never been invited into her place, either.

When Mark Colby eventually defected to Moscow there had been another visit from a man from Broadway House. Had she ever heard from Colby since she left? Was there anything about his behaviour when she worked for him that seemed odd or suspicious? He didn't make notes or seem all that interested in her answers. Like the others, he said it was just routine. It had been enough to make her delay saying "yes" to John. But they had married a year later.

The years went by uneventfully. They never talked about having children and, although his love-making was infrequent, she knew that he understood that she didn't want a family. He was an undemanding man and never pressed the point.

She frequently thought about the little girl. Wondering if she was happy. When it rained she hoped she was properly wrapped up, and at Christmas and on her birthday she shed hot tears of shame and guilt and something that wasn't love but was very like it. Many times she thought of trying to trace the girl but she had signed the piece of paper, and anyway she didn't want to risk hurting John. There was an inertia that seemed too great to overcome. And a fear of the consequences of any action she might take.

She had barely heard the clerk of the court reading out the charges of blackmail on Mr X, and then the petty thefts and frauds, because she was so shocked at the sight of the prisoner in the dock. She had always thought of her as a girl. But she was a woman. A woman in her forties. Pale-faced, unkempt hair, an ungainly body and those staring blue eyes. His eyes. She had left the courtroom hurriedly and found a small café where she had a coffee as she tried to collect her thoughts. Her daughter looked older than she did herself. She couldn't identify with the strange wild figure in the dock between the two policewomen.

An hour later she had gone back to the court and asked the usher outside the courtroom when the case would be over. He thought it would take three days.

She had to keep to the story she had told John about going to Southend each day for a breath of sea air but she had wandered the streets of London, seeing nothing.

After lunch on the last day the judge was to pass sentence and she sat listening to his words and then the outburst from the sad figure in the dock.

It was a week after the court case that the man called. He showed her his ID card and she let him in. He was a good-looking man in his forties in a well-cut dark-blue suit.

'I just wanted to check that you were satisfied with how we dealt with the blackmail business. I can assure you that it won't happen again.'

'I don't understand. What blackmail business?'

The surprise on his face was unmistakably genuine but he moved in the armchair as if he was just uncomfortably seated. When he looked back at her face he was composed again.

'I'm sorry, Mrs Palmer. I've obviously made a mistake.'

She shook her head. 'I don't think so. Tell me why you're here. I want to know.'

'Your husband obviously wanted to protect you from any pressure.'

'My husband?' She looked amazed. 'What do you mean?'

'He didn't mention it to you?'

'Mention what?'

The man sighed and glanced away for a moment before he looked back at her. 'Mrs Palmer, there has obviously been some confusion. Let me tell you what happened.' He paused. 'The lady, Mary Lewis, obtained your identity. We are not sure how but we think it was from a KGB officer. She has always been under routine surveillance because of her father. We pulled in the KGB officer who contacted her, to interrogate him. It seems that Mary Lewis wrote many letters over the years to her father. Letters that became pretty desperate. They were read, of course, by the KGB before they were handed over to Colby. He ignored them and it seems that this KGB man was not an admirer of friend Colby. He felt it was heartless to ignore the girl, the woman. She first wrote when she was still in the orphanage. The KGB man thought it might help the girl if he met her or even tried to help her. He has children of his own and it seems the thought of the abandoned girl upset him.

'Anyway, to cut a longish story short, the KGB man gave her your married name and your address. She sent your husband a letter threatening to sell her story to the press unless he paid her a sum of money. It started at a thousand pounds and came down to five hundred. Your husband, quite rightly, took it to the police who passed it on to us. As you know, the woman was dealt with in court.' He shrugged. 'That's about it.'

'You mean John was the Mr X?'

'Yes. But, as you know, the details of the blackmail were not mentioned in court. They never are in blackmail cases.'

'Why didn't John tell me?'

'He was much concerned that you should not be upset. I'm sure that was the only reason.'

'So he knows about Colby and the rest of it?'

'Yes.'

'Was he angry or upset?'

'No. Not at all. He was just angry that you had been so badly treated. That was all.'

'What on earth shall I say to him?'

'I think it would be best if you left things as they are and said nothing.'

'And you won't tell him that I know?'
'Of course not, if that's what you want.'
'Yes,' she said softly, 'that's what I want.'

She stood looking out of the bedroom window, watching him as he walked up the road from the station with Harris from next-door-but-one. He was smiling as they chatted, his tie flapping around in the wind. John Palmer, the man she thought was so ordinary, so unimaginative. A man who didn't bring her flowers and never said he loved her. No easy charm and no twinkling blue eyes. But worth a thousand Colbys.

THE PARTY OF THE SECOND PART

———

Brewster had been managing clerk for the chambers ever since he came back from the war. He knew the skills and vagaries of his principals like a farmer knows his dairy herd. When he knocked on the door marked "Mathew Porter" he stepped into the QC's office with the brief held firmly in his hand. The lawyer was scribbling notes on his pad, one hand keeping open one of the bound Law Reports for 1938. He glanced up at Brewster and pointed to a space on his desk with his gold pencil.

'Stick it down there, Brewster, please.'

'I thought I'd better have a word with you about it, sir. It's from Mr Maclean.'

'What is it?'

'Defence of a divorce petition.'

Porter shook his head. 'You know I never do Family Court cases. Give it to Mr Henry.'

'Mr Maclean insisted it should be you, sir.'

'He ought to know better, he's been dealing with us for long enough.'

'Quite, sir. He gives the chambers a lot of work. That's why I hesitated to refuse the brief. But he says you'd understand when you'd perused it.'

Porter leaned back in his chair, looking at Brewster. 'Don't use words like peruse to me Brewster. You sound like a City of London copper first time in court. I don't peruse the bloody things. I read 'em.'

'It was Mr Maclean's word, sir.'

Porter laughed. 'OK, I'll have a look at it but you'll have to

121

pass it over to our Henry.' He paused and reached for a pack of Gauloises. 'Why does he want me to take it?'

'The party was in Special Operations Executive during the war. That was your mob, wasn't it, sir?'

Porter raised his eyebrows. 'Leave it with me. I'll talk to Maclean myself when I've read it.'

'Right you are, sir.'

'What's the defendant's name, by the way?' He leaned forward and looked at the brief. It said "Pryke v. Pryke". 'Pryke. I don't recognise the name. Was he in the French Section?'

'No idea, sir. It's not a chap, it's a woman.'

'OK. Leave it with me.'

Mathew Porter read through the brief and agreed to have lunch with Maclean at the Law Society. They were neither of them great social chatterers and Porter got down to business as soon as they had ordered.

'I wanted to have a word with you about that Pryke brief. It's not my kind of thing you know, Jamie. I never do divorces. Why not let Henry take it over? He's the expert.'

Maclean smiled. 'Have you read the brief?'

'Of course.'

'What did you think of it?'

'Not a cat in hell's chance. Can't see why she's defending it. If her husband can substantiate half what he alleges, she's wasting her time and ours. And her money too.'

'She's got a fantastic war record, Mathew. OBE and Legion of Honour from the French. I thought you might have a fellow feeling. Comrades in arms, and all that.'

'I say. This soup is terribly salty. Comrades in arms, you say.' He paused with the spoon raised to his lips. 'You know, SOE wasn't like a regiment. Too dispersed. Loyalties were very local and personal.' He sighed. 'Apart from all that they were a very mixed bunch. Couldn't say that there were more than half a dozen I'd like to see again. Who's been briefed for the other side?'

'Lowther. Sir Geoffrey himself.'

'Why the big guns? I'd have thought the plaintiff would sail through this. Why the hell does she want to defend anyway?'

'Two reasons, I think. First, she doesn't believe in divorce and secondly, she was staggered at the stuff they were using against her.'

'What's she like?'

'A nice woman. Quiet, but plenty of guts. Intelligent and well-educated. And quite attractive.'

'I'd have advised her to cut her losses. Call it a day.' He smiled. 'Plenty of other fish in the sea and all that.'

'I feel she's being put upon, Mathew. Blackmailed almost.'

'How do you make that out?'

'I think I could have persuaded her to let it go through until she saw the other side's accusations. That really put her hackles up. And the husband's a poor specimen, anyway.'

'Why do you say that?'

'No decent chap would want to throw this sort of muck at a woman like her. She doesn't deserve it, believe me.'

Porter smiled. 'Sounds like you've got a soft spot for her, Jamie.'

'I have. She was a heroine and she's being abused for it.'

'Was the husband in the services during the war?'

'No. He was some minor civil servant at the War Office. That's how he met her. He was her escort to the Palace when she was presented with her medal. Fell madly in love with her. Swept her off her feet and now he turns on her.' He dabbed his lips with a paper napkin. 'I thought I might persuade you to put up a bit of a fight on her behalf. As things are she'll lose but she deserves a helping hand.'

'All anybody can do is make the other side look as unpleasant as they really are. Henry could do that better than I can. I'm not much of an advocate. Industrial courts don't like advocates. Just precedents.'

'Would you have a word with her? Just a quick conference. For me, Mathew.'

Porter smiled. 'Of course I will, Jamie. How about you send her over to me tomorrow about three?'

Maclean smiled. 'I won't forget it. Thanks.'

'You said just now – "as things stand, she'll lose". What did you mean?'

'Did I say that? Well, I shouldn't have. Talking out of turn.'

'Come on. Out with it.'

'You won't mention this to her, will you?'

'Not if you say I shouldn't.'

'She knows something about him that could knock his whole case down. The real reason why he wants the marriage finished. She won't let me use it. Made me promise.'

'Do you know what it is?'

123

'Yes.'

'Tell me.'

'I can't. I promised. I did a bit of rooting around on this fellow Pryke and came across this . . . fact, let's call it. I told her about it but she already knew. Flew off the handle at me for being a busybody. Said that using it would make her no better than him. She's right of course, but by God I'd have used it.'

'Give me a clue.'

'Don't tempt me, Mathew.'

Porter laughed. 'An indirect clue.'

For a few moments Maclean sat silent and then he opened his mouth to speak, hesitated and then closed his mouth. Porter waited. Then Maclean said, 'Think of the reasons why he might not have been called up in the war.'

Porter shrugged. 'I'll think about it. Tomorrow at three.'

She wasn't at all what Porter had expected. She was prettier. Forty-ish but with one of those faces whose bone structure would always make her look younger than her years. She wore a summer dress that gave her an almost schoolgirlish air of innocence. The grey-blue eyes looked at him calmly but the tension showed in her tight-clasped hands.

He didn't refer to her husband's statement but talked about what she hoped for by defending the action.

She shrugged. 'I'd just like somebody who believes in me to make me seem less of a . . . harridan . . . than they're trying to make me out.'

'I could call people from SOE, or use their records to establish that you were very brave and operated in enemy-occupied territory.'

'I wouldn't want them dragged in. The publicity will be bad enough, whatever I say. And I don't want to pose as a heroine.'

'But you were.'

She laughed softly. 'You were in SOE, so you know better than that. The heroines were burnt in the ovens at Mauthausen and Ravensbrück.'

'You didn't get an OBE for just sitting around in the Dordogne.'

She shook her head. 'The things I did were done in desperation. I'm a natural born coward, not a heroine.'

'Mr Maclean asked me to take the brief but I must point out that I'm not a divorce lawyer and that could be to your disadvantage.'

'I'd still be grateful if you took it on.'

'Why?'

'Because you were in SOE and I'll know that there's one other person in court who knows what it was all about.' She smiled. 'Somebody to wear my lace hankie on his lance.'

Porter smiled and stood up. 'All right. On your head be it. I'll phone Jamie Maclean and tell him I'll act for you.'

She was trembling as he walked her to the outer office and he went back to his own office and picked up the phone.

'Get me Colonel Ramage, please. His number's in our book. It might be under War Office Records or the Military Secretary's office . . . thank you.'

Standing in the court corridors always lowered clients' morale and he took her down to the canteen until they were called.

She was wearing a pale blue two-piece suit and a frilly blouse. No attempt to impress the court with a sombre appearance.

'What can we talk about?' she said as she stirred her coffee.

'What's your favourite piece of music?'

She laughed. 'Either Josephine Baker singing "*J'ai deux amours*" or the Mendelssohn fiddle concerto.'

'Favourite flower?'

'Daisies in a field. Marguerites.'

'Favourite food?'

'Chocolate eclairs.' She laughed.

'And favourite book?'

'Elizabeth Smart's *By Grand Central Station I Sat Down and Wept*.'

And then Maclean came for them and the grimness of the corridors set her trembling again.

Porter sat listening, watching her face as the questions were put to her. Sir Geoffrey was silky and polite but he was there to do a job. A demolition job.

'You admit that you abused your husband on occasions, using foul language.'

'No, I don't admit anything of the sort.'

Sir Geoffrey raised his ginger eyebrows in surprise as he looked at his notes. 'But you have already agreed that you said . . . "You lying sod, get out of my sight." Wouldn't you say that was foul language?'

'I was angry at something he'd done. He'd . . .'

'Thank you, Mrs Pryke. Now let me come to the question of violence.' Sir Geoffrey looked up quickly at her. 'Are you a violent woman, Mrs Pryke? Do you have a violent temper?'

'I can be tormented into being angry, if that's what you call violence.'

'Have you ever struck your husband, Mrs Pryke?'

'I slapped his face once. Nothing more than that.'

'Did he ever strike you?'

'No.'

'I see. But when you – as you put it – slapped his face, it was with sufficient force to injure his eye. Yes?'

'It cracked his contact lens. That's all.'

'Causing damage enough to keep him from his office for ten days.'

'That was the time it took to replace the lens. Nothing more.'

'Of course not.' Sir Geoffrey smiled at the jury. 'Just a wifely love tap.' Then Sir Geoffrey's voice was very soft as he looked at her. 'I must ask you one last question, Mrs Pryke. I want you to listen very carefully.' Sir Geoffrey glanced at the jury and then back at the witness box. 'Mrs Pryke. Have you ever killed a man?'

Porter saw the blood drain from her face and her knuckles were white as they grasped the edge of the box. Then she said quietly, 'Yes. But that was . . .'

'Mrs Pryke, how many men have you killed in your lifetime?'

She took a deep breath. 'Two, and in both cases . . .'

'Thank you, Mrs Pryke. And one last question to you. In the case of one of the men you killed, you used a pistol. What did you use in the other case?'

'I used a knife.'

'You stabbed him several times? Three or four times, perhaps?'

'I don't remember.'

'I see.' Sir Geoffrey raised his eyebrows in the general direction of the Press benches. 'That will be all, thank you, Mrs Pryke.'

Mathew Porter stood up slowly. 'My Lord, I know we are already running late but after my learned colleague's last few questions I should like a few moments more so that this matter does not hang over the night.'

His Lordship nodded. 'Don't be too long, Mr Porter, but carry on.'

Porter turned to his client. 'Mrs Pryke, would you tell the court who the two men were whom you killed.'

'I don't remember their names.'

'Their ranks, perhaps. Or the circumstances.'

'One was a Gestapo officer and one was a sergeant in the Sicherheitsdienst. The Nazi Security Service.'

'Tell us very briefly what happened.'

'They had arrested the seven leading people in my SOE network. I killed the two men to set my colleagues free.'

'This was in war-time? In German-occupied France?'

'Yes.'

'And for this you were awarded the Order of the British Empire. You received it from King George the Sixth himself at Buckingham Palace.'

'Yes.'

'And was the plaintiff, your husband, aware of these facts even before he married you?'

'Yes. He accompanied me to the medal presentation.'

'Thank you, Mrs Pryke.' Porter turned to look at the Judge. 'My Lord, tomorrow I should like to suggest to the court that this application is dismissed on the grounds that the evidence put forward to denigrate my client's character has been done with deliberate malice and was to a large part intended to create both a totally false impression of the real facts and an attempt to deceive the court . . .'

'Mr Porter. Can we leave the rest of it until tomorrow at ten?'

'As your Lordship pleases.'

Porter and Maclean had walked over to the Wig and Pen with their client and taken a table at the far end. She seemed to have recovered from her nervousness.

'Thanks for what you said. About the SOE business.'

'I ought not to have needed to say it. It was a scurrilous attack on their part and I'm surprised that Sir Geoffrey would wear it. The rest was pretty thin but to my mind that last bit went too far. I don't think His Lordship liked it too much. What do you think, Jamie?'

Maclean grinned. 'I'd say there's a good chance of them throwing it out tomorrow.'

Jill Pryke looked at Maclean. 'Does that mean he might not get a divorce?'

'It's quite possible, my dear, and I'd think you might even be able to consider bringing a cross-petition citing today as your reason.'

As they chatted Porter was aware of his client's silence and eventually he said, 'What's the problem?'

She took a deep breath. 'I want to withdraw. Let it be undefended.'

'But why?'

'I don't want to be married to him any more.'

'You can cross-petition, like I said.'

'That would take time. I'd like to be free of him tomorrow.'

Porter looked at Maclean who said, 'Think about it overnight. Don't rush into it.'

She shook her head as she looked at Porter. 'Don't think I'm not grateful. I am. Terribly grateful. But hearing you sticking up for me in court was enough. I felt hounded, but not any more. I just want to be free of it. All of it.'

Maclean said, 'If you're sure that's what you want.'

'It is,' she said as she stood up. 'I'd like to leave while I feel happy, if you don't mind.'

She shook hands with Porter and Maclean walked her into the Strand, waved down a taxi for her and walked back to Porter at the table.

'My God. Human beings. What a turmoil we're always in.'

Porter smiled. 'She's right, you know. She should have gone this way right at the start. She's only doing what we both counselled her to do. But she's had her bite back in court. And why shouldn't she?' He paused and looked at Maclean. 'I didn't realise until this afternoon what her little secret was that you wouldn't let me know.'

'OK. Why this afternoon?'

Porter smiled. 'Watching Sir Geoffrey. He was loving every minute of it. Hounding her. Hating her. They're two of a kind, aren't they, him and Pryke? Brothers in sex?'

Maclean nodded. 'He made a declaration when he was called up about his . . . er . . . predilections. That's why he wasn't in the services. The marriage must have been hopeless from the start.'

'Ah well. All's well that ends well.'

The small boy was looking at the things on the table.

'What's the music, Daddy?'

'It's a violin concerto by a chap named Mendelssohn.'

'What a funny name.'

'It isn't really, it's just a foreign name.'

'And you always give her these things as well as a proper

present. Why eclairs and a bunch of daisies and always this same book?'

'A long time ago we sat in a rather gloomy tea place and I asked her about her favourite things. These were the things she chose.'

'Were you two married then?'

'No. It was a long time ago.'

'Did you like her when you had tea with her?'

'I admired her. I got to like her later.'

'Why?'

'Oh, lots of reasons. I'll tell you some day when I've worked out what they are. She's coming in from the garden now. Thinks we've forgotten her birthday.'

The small boy smiled. 'Women are funny, aren't they?'

This story was first published in the 1984 anthology, Winter's Crimes 16, *edited by Hilary Hale.*

THE DANDLED DAYS

Like truthless dreams, so are my joys expired;
And past return are all my dandled days;
My love misled, and fancy quite retired:
Of all which past the sorrow only stays.

Walter de la Mare

The press notice had said that he'd been offered Birmingham Town Hall for the concert but he'd insisted that it should be at the Hippodrome. Dear old Hippodrome, still smelling faintly of Jeyes Fluid on the stairs, but the place that they had gone to in the old days to see the big bands: Roy Fox, Lew Stone, Ambrose, Geraldo and all the rest of them. When the big Paul Whiteman Band had come over from America, there were so many of them to fit on stage that you could only see the feet of the back row below the proscenium.

The wild applause started all over again as the spotlight picked him out as he walked from the wings to the microphone in front of the band. He was looking up at the gallery, smiling, and the audience fell silent as he spoke.

'. . . It's been lovely being with you all tonight . . . thank you for coming.' He shrugged and paused, 'And now . . . there's only one thing I can say . . .'

There was a moment's silence and then, as he sang the first words of "Moonlight and Roses" to the band's lush accompaniment, there was a swell of enthusiastic applause that slowly died away so that they could hear the words and the music of his much-loved signature tune.

It was twenty-five years since she last saw him. Twenty-five years, four months and two days. And he didn't look older. More mature, maybe. But the smile was the same, and the brown eyes. And even now his hair was still black.

She didn't wait for the end. She wasn't sure why.

In his dressing-room old Walt, his dresser, had a warm lemon and honey ready for him and he was sipping it slowly when there was a knock at the door.

'That'll be young Lawson from the *Birmingham Mail*, Dave . . . shall I let him in?'

'OK. Fine.'

He stood up as the young man came in. 'Hello, Mr Lawson . . . do sit down . . . a whisky?'

'Not for me, sir, thank you all the same.'

'Well, make yourself comfortable.' He paused. 'Now what can I do for you, Mr Lawson?'

'The paper's going to do a special article on you, sir. Not just tonight's show but a general-interest piece.'

'Is it now? What is it you want to know?'

'You were born here in Birmingham, weren't you?'

'I was.'

'Where were you born?'

'I've no idea. I was dumped on the steps of the police station when I was two weeks old. The orphanage took me in and brought me up.'

'Was it because you were an orphanage boy that you came back to do the charity show for the orphanage tonight?'

'Yes. I guess so.'

'When you left the orphanage and had a job, where did you live?'

'In Victoria Road, Aston, and later on I had a room in Erdington.'

'When did you leave Birmingham?'

He hesitated as he worked it out. '. . . In . . . 1938. First of August, 1938 – just over twenty-five years ago.'

'You've never been back since then . . . until tonight?'

'That's right.'

'Why so long?'

'I had no reason to come back.'

'By the way, the manager of the Hippodrome told me that the show tonight raised fifteen thousand pounds for the orphanage.'

'Jolly good.'

'The manager also told me that you'd had many invitations to perform here but you'd always refused. I wondered why you'd not wanted to come back, even for a professional engagement.'

'Maybe they couldn't agree terms with my agent.'

'Somebody told me that you never came back because of something that happened when you lived here.'

'Did they now . . . and what else did they tell you?'

Lawson said quietly, 'They said you left here because of an unhappy love affair . . . and it sort of put you against the place.'

'What else do you want to ask me?'

'It's a kind of romantic story, Mr Maxwell. Are you sure . . .?'

David Maxwell shook his head. 'It isn't a romantic story, I can assure you. It was a lot of things . . . but it wasn't that.'

'Who was she . . . the girl?'

'She was just a girl. A working-class girl.'

'What was your job in those days?'

'I was a labourer, a moulder's labourer in a foundry.'

'Does the girl still live here?'

'I've no idea.'

'You didn't keep in touch with her, then?'

'No.' He paused. 'I'm sorry, but I've got a business meeting back at the hotel. I'll have to throw you out now.'

'I hope I haven't offended you. Would you autograph my programme for me?'

'Of course I will.' He smiled. 'At least you didn't say it was for your mother . . . there you are, lad.'

'Thanks, Dave . . . very nice talking to you.'

When the young reporter had left, old Walt said, 'I didn't know you had any appointments tonight, Dave.'

'I haven't. I just wanted to get rid of him . . . give me the cream so I can get this muck off my face.'

She put the breakfast things in the sink, poured herself another coffee and took it over to the kitchen table. As she stirred the coffee her thoughts were a long way away.

She wondered what they would think if they knew. Mary Logan: wife, mother and general dogsbody. Forty-five, solid and reliable; occupation, housewife. She wondered what Dave would think if he could see her now. The girl who was going to be famous and sing with Roy Fox's band . . . Al Bowlly and Denny Dennis and her.

The family wouldn't believe it, and Dave – he wouldn't recognise her. Wouldn't want to, either . . . and she couldn't blame him.

She could remember the very first time they met – She'd won the ladies' talent contest at a works dance. And David Maxwell had won the gents' prize. She'd sung "Moonlight and Roses". It was her song in those days. Her party piece. Dave had sung "I'm in the Mood for Love".

He walked her back home that night. David Maxwell, eighteen years old. A year older than her. She lived in Kingsbury Road then, with Mum and Dad, and Dave must have had a long walk back to Aston. He asked if he could see her the next Saturday. He said he'd take her to the dance at the Masonic. Boys didn't generally offer to take a girl to a dance. It meant paying for the girl as well – they generally suggested meeting them inside. It was a shilling to go in those days and paying for the girl as well could leave the chap broke for the rest of the week. It was like Dad's favourite description of courting – "When a tuppenny bun costs fourpence".

She'd said she'd meet him inside and he looked relieved. She went with Maggie and they were playing "Robins and Roses" when they took their seats along the side of the wall.

In those days it was quite formal at those local hops. Most of the boys wore proper patent leather dancing shoes – they put french chalk on the floors to make them smooth – and the band played three numbers and then the fellow took the girl back to where she had been sitting with her friends. And although they were only working-class chaps, they were polite when they asked a girl to dance – 'May I have the pleasure?' and all that.

You didn't have to be pretty to get asked for a dance – although the pretty girls were asked first, of course – but girls who were quite plain but could dance well were kept dancing all evening with somebody.

That night she danced most of the time with Dave and she picked him for the "ladies' excuse-me". And they danced the last waltz together.

When a fellow asked a girl for the last waltz it was a kind of signal that he liked the girl and, if she accepted, the boy would walk her home. Nothing much happened on the walk home, of course. Maybe holding hands or an arm round a waist, maybe even a peck on the cheek when they said goodnight.

Not long after they met, Dave had joined a local dance band as their vocalist, and she used to go with him on Wednesday nights to the rehearsals.

She'd liked Dave, but she thought at first that he was a rather touchy young man. Even the mildest word of criticism and he'd go all silent. Not rude – just silent and closed-up. It wasn't until the Christmas of that year that she learned from somebody at work that he had been abandoned as a baby by his parents and had been brought up in the orphanage. It really upset her when she was told. She was sorry about the times when she'd snapped back at him and he'd gone into his shell. No wonder he was touchy, with a background like that.

It was about this time that Mum discovered she'd got a regular boy-friend. She said all the usual things – she was too young to be thinking about steady boy-friends and, from what she'd heard, he wasn't the kind she should be spending her time with, anyway. She'd told her about the orphanage bit to make her mother sympathetic towards him, but she wasn't the sympathetic type. She supposed it was the first time in her life when she knew for certain that she didn't really like her own mother. They'd never got on all that well and she'd realised long before that she took after her dad, not her mum. The difference was that Dad never had a bad word to say about anybody. And Mum never had a good one.

Because she worked in the wages office she knew how much everybody earned. Well, not the foremen and the bosses. But the workers. Dave did a forty-four hour week, including Saturday mornings, and he got thirty-seven shillings a week. His landlady took twenty-five shillings so, with two shillings deductions, it left ten shillings for clothes, fares and entertainment. He didn't complain. Nobody did in those days. That was how it was and they just got on with it. For those who lived at home it meant a bit more spending money but somehow they envied the ones who were independent, who could do what they wanted and come home as late as they wanted.

She gave him a scarf for Christmas. And that scarf was a sort of turning point. For two reasons. First of all she had to stay at home on Christmas Day but she'd walked down to Salford Bridge to meet him. He'd had to walk much further from Aston. And when he opened his parcel he looked away, towards the canal. There were tears in his eyes. She found out later that it was the first time in his life that somebody had given him a present. They stood talking at the tram stop for nearly half an hour. There were no trams that day because it was Christmas Day, and it was bitterly cold. When it was time to go she put her arms round his shoulders and gave him a proper kiss. And then she'd stood there and watched him walk away. He didn't look back, or wave, or anything, and she was both sad and happy as she walked back up the hill.

She'd known Dave for nearly a year before she was allowed to bring him home for tea. Her mother was at her worst. You'd have thought he was up before the beak, the way she questioned him – he was quite capable of sticking up for himself, but she knew he didn't like it. She was one of those women who bowed and scraped to anybody who had a car or a radiogram – and people like doctors and parsons. She had a special voice she put on – very posh – and you'd have thought she was royalty when she was talking to those she saw as her equals or inferiors. There was no doubt she saw Dave as an inferior. Her mother had asked her the next day if she'd noticed his dirty hands – and she'd told her mother what she thought of her behaviour the day before. Dave had big hands like Dad's and, like Dad's, they were both strong and gentle and you could have soaked them in bleach for a week and it'd have made no difference. If you work in a foundry the black sand gradually works its way into all the creases and under your nails until it's part of your hands. Mum knew that, of course.

She apologised to Dave for how Mum had been. He said he hadn't noticed anything – but she knew he had. But they got one laugh out of it. He borrowed a record from a mate of his and she left her door open when she played it. It was Jack Buchanan singing "And Her Mother Came Too".

Dave talked the chap who ran the band into giving her an audition. It meant that, if he liked her singing, she would be singing with Dave at the Saturday night dances. She hardly slept the night before, she was so excited. She could remember it so well, even now.

Stan, the bandleader, said she was OK – she'd get ten shillings a night, which was pretty good. Dave got thirty shillings a night but he was much more experienced and he was a much better singer than she was. People came to the Saturday hops from other parts of town just because he was the vocalist. Sometimes they just stopped dancing and stood by the platform, listening. He used to look at her while he was singing and everybody knew she was his girl . . . she loved it.

Looking back, it seemed terribly pathetic. An amateur dance

band in the draughty Masonic hall in a Birmingham suburb with most of the dancers there because it was only half the price of dancing at the Palais, where the manager wore a dinner jacket.

Eight to eleven and then the last waltz and something to keep them happy as they got their street clothes on. She guessed that all over the country that last tune was the same – "Goodnight, Sweetheart".

Most Saturday nights she did four vocals and Dave did six or seven and in their hearts they hoped they'd be talent-spotted from someone at the Palais. They never admitted it, of course . . . it would have seemed disloyal to old Stan whom everybody respected because he had once been the pianist at a posh London hotel.

When the big chance came it wasn't from the Palais, it was from one of the big dance halls in town. In fact they didn't call themselves a dance hall, it was a ballroom. A full-sized band and full-time – every day except Sundays. It was Dave they wanted, of course. Seven pounds a week and clothes money for a dinner jacket suit. It was fantastic money for those days. She could remember sitting in the posh office with the man who owned the place as he talked it over with Dave. And she could remember the look on the chap's face as Dave dropped the bombshell. He'd accept the offer only if they took her on as well. Dave hadn't discussed it with her beforehand and it was a bit embarrassing sitting there. The chap obviously wasn't interested in her at all but he was desperate to get Dave. In the end he said he'd take the two of them on for ten pounds. Seven for Dave, three for her. She didn't remember either of them asking her if she agreed, but she signed the contract and that was that. They stayed on afterwards and had a dance or two. Dave asked the band to play what was her favourite at the time – "Please". She'd still got the Bing Crosby version of it.

She'd thought that her parents would be as pleased as she was. She ought to have known better. Dad was pleased, but a bit worried about her giving up what he saw as a steady job, but Mum had done a bit of quick arithmetic. With ten pounds a week, Dave and Mary could get married and have a place of their own. It wasn't even in their minds then but she guessed that they'd get around to it sooner or later. And she was determined to stop them. There was row after row, day after day. The ballroom was made into a den of iniquity. She'd come to a bad end. That was for Dad's benefit and it went home, all right. It was all Dave's doing. She said he wanted to get her in his power – shades of Ruby M. Ayres.

It sounded funny now but it wasn't funny then. Silent meals

or constant nagging. Dave had moved to Erdington a couple of months before and he'd got a room on Slade Road. Mum had the cheek to go down to see his landlady. Telling her the tale. But she got a cold reception there. The minister at the Congregational – even the doctor – were all dragged into it. She thought the minister was rather taken with the idea – he'd had ambitions to go on the stage when he was young. The more her mother went on about it the more determined she had been to do it. She gave in her notice and the office gave her a manicure set as a leaving present, and she wondered how long it would take for her to be singing for Roy Fox. But the first song she sang with the band was a Ray Noble number called "By the Fireside". They didn't do it quite as smoothly as the real thing.

She only had one week at the ballroom. Dave and she had gone to Sutton Park on his Tuesday off and they'd had tea at a café in the town afterwards. Then they went to the cinema. There was a re-run of a Fred Astaire-Ginger Rogers film. They'd got several Fred Astaire records but their favourite was "A Fine Romance".

She supposed that day was the happiest day of her life. When they were sitting in the bus-stop Dave had asked her to marry him. And she said yes.

She'd often wondered if they had just gone straight back home, would things have turned out differently? It obviously wouldn't have changed anything but she used to feel guilty about not having been there. But they went back to the Parade. The shops were closed but there were lights in the window of the jewellery shop. They must have stayed for about half an hour looking at the rings and then they decided to walk back instead of taking a bus. It was just after eleven when they got back and as soon as she got in she knew that something had happened. There were no lights on and the fire had gone out. When the doorbell rang she sent Dave to answer it. It was a policeman. She felt faint. She heard them talking in the hall and then Dave came in with the policeman. Mum and Dad had been hit by a car while they were crossing the road by the bank at Six Ways, and they'd been taken to the General Hospital in Steelhouse Lane. Dad had died in the ambulance and Mum was seriously injured. When she saw her in the hospital bed she knew that everything was going to be changed. She'd been terribly knocked about . . . but it wasn't that. It was how she looked . . . she looked like a child . . . small and frail, and the blue eyes staring into space . . . lost.

It was six weeks before she came back home. They'd done a good job but she needed two walking sticks to get herself around. She didn't complain . . . she'd got a lot of courage. And despite her mother's attitude in the past, she felt a tremendous sympathy for her. Mum had found it difficult to speak but she knew she was grateful that she was looking after her. She didn't want to tell her mother about Dave and her until she was much better and capable of coping with the situation. It was the end of her job with the band and for a long time it meant no job at all.

Dave came in every afternoon before he had to go off to town in the evening. Except on Wednesdays when there was a tea-dance at the ballroom. She hated Wednesdays. There was a song that matched her mood in those days called "Saturday Night is the Loneliest Night of the Week".

Mum kept out of the way when Dave was around. And gradually life settled down to a kind of routine. Most days she coped but sometimes she was terribly depressed because she couldn't see any end to the sheer monotony of dealing with a frail old woman who was so dependent on her. Dave told her the gossip about the fellows in the band but neither of them talked any more about being engaged or being married. Just once they went out together. A neighbour had offered to sit-in for her and they went to the pictures. On a Sunday. It was *Love Finds Andy Hardy*. Tame enough, you'd think, but she had a guilt complex as long as your arm. Not about leaving Mum but because of going to the cinema on a Sunday. She'd never done that before and nowadays nobody would believe how terrible it seemed. Even now she can never hear Judy Garland sing anything without remembering that guilty feeling.

Christmas came and went, and then Easter and summer, and nothing changed. At least she thought it hadn't changed. Dave came to tea on the Sunday. She knew something was up as soon as she saw him but he didn't break the news until they had settled down after tea. He'd been offered a three-year contract by one of the big London bands that played every night at a luxury hotel. She thought he said it was called the Dorchester but she didn't really remember. The pay was incredible – forty pounds a week. It seemed hard to imagine how you could spend that kind of money, let alone earn it. What Dave wanted was that they got married in the next few weeks and they'd set up house together in London. He'd already found a place for them. He hadn't mentioned Mum and when she asked about her he said they would be able to afford somebody full-time to look after her in her own surroundings. She asked him if she could think about it and although he said yes, she thought he'd taken it for granted that she'd leap at the chance. When he was leaving that night, she asked him what would happen if she said no. He said it would make no difference as far as he was concerned. He'd wait but obviously, with him being in London, they wouldn't see very much of one another.

He came up about once a month, staying at a hotel at the tram terminus at Chester Road. Mum was pretty well bed-ridden by then. It was safe to leave her for about half an hour and they'd walk down the road. Dave had a car by then – a Standard. It was gorgeous – that smell of new leather. They would go for a short drive and buy some cakes for tea. The week before the August Bank Holiday he had four days off. He spent most of the time with her and she thought all was going well. It was a wonderful change for her, having him around. But on the Sunday it all went wrong – it was her own fault. He'd bought her a beautiful ring and said he thought it was time they got married. He said she was getting old before her time, living her kind of life. He said she was a victim – a willing victim. Throwing her life away.

She supposed she'd known it couldn't go on but she'd refused to face the facts up to then. She was hoping for something to happen, some sign that would tell her what to do. But there hadn't been a sign. She knew in her mind that Dave was right but in her heart of hearts she knew she couldn't do it. She said she'd think about it overnight and they'd talk again the next day. She saw as she said it how disappointed he was. She took Mum up some warm milk before she went to bed and she looked at her lying there. Mum was only a bit older than she was right now but she looked so small and thin and wrinkled. The wisps of hair and the washed-out blue eyes that followed her everywhere without her moving her head. Down in the kitchen she rehearsed a hundred times the words she would use to break it to her. To explain how it would be better for her. And she knew she'd never do it. She'd never be able to bring herself to do it. Maybe they could work out some alternative. She put on her favourite records and sat listening before she went up to bed.

She hardly slept at all that night and about seven she came down in her dressing-gown to make a cup of tea. She saw the letter on the inside mat. It was far too early for the post. It just had her name on it – Mary Bailey – and it was Dave's handwriting. She stood in the hall reading it. It wasn't very long. He said he'd waited and waited for over a year. He realised that what it amounted to was choosing between him and her mother and he knew now that Mum would always come before him. He loved her and admired her strength of character but it wasn't going to work out for the two of them. He'd always see her as a friend and she could count on him too as a friend. He wouldn't pester her any more.

It was August Bank Holiday Monday but she felt as cold as ice. She went around in a daze and it was two weeks before she could think about it sensibly. She knew from the words in his letter that she'd hurt him deeply. In his eyes she'd abandoned him, just like his parents had done when he was a baby. She hadn't, of course. She loved him and she'd never even liked any other man. To her they were a pair and that was that. She'd been very stupid not to realise what he was feeling. She'd taken him for granted. It didn't matter that he was wrong. It was what he'd thought that mattered. She was twenty-one and she had felt like an old woman. There's a tune that always reminded her of those times. Even now it upset her to hear it. But she often played it when she was on her own. It was called "Smoke Gets in Your Eyes".

She heard Dave singing with Lew Stone's band as guest vocalist one night about six months later. It was on the wireless. It was live from some West End hotel and he got lots of applause. She wondered how he was getting on in his new life. And she wondered if he had a new girl. The next time she heard him on the radio was the Saturday night before Chamberlain declared war on Germany. She couldn't remember most of what he sang but he did sing "Moonlight and Roses". He'd announced that it was his signature tune. Those first five months of the war were an odd sort of time. Nothing much happened and food wasn't all that short.

Because she had to look after Mum she wasn't really involved in the war at all. The Air-Raid Warden used to knock on the door to see they were all right when there was a raid on. They'd put one of those Morrison shelters in the front room but she'd never used it. Mum was too far gone to be disturbed by the bombs or the sirens. She survived on broth and biscuits and sometimes she fancied a bit of Spam. As for herself, she hardly knew what day it was. It made no difference to her whether it was Monday or Saturday apart from the dates on the ration cards. The butcher was very good to them. Saved them offal like liver and kidneys and sometimes he got them a few fresh eggs. They had a very bad raid in the November. The night after they bombed Coventry. She was really scared that night, even Mum could hear the explosions. She told her it was a gas main but she didn't think she understood what was going on.

She got a card from Dave that Christmas with a Yorkshire postmark. He was in the army. And a month later there was a knock on the door and there he was in his battle-dress, smiling. He'd got a week's embarkation leave. And after all they'd been through it seemed quite normal to see him again. He stayed for a long weekend. Several neighbours took turns looking after Mum and they had trips out each day. They went to Lichfield on the Midland Red, and to Malvern, and they had tea at the Gaumont in town. And all that was just to put off remembering the rest.

It was the first time she'd ever slept with a man. It wasn't very romantic in that tiny bedroom with the damp patches on the wall and the sagging bed. And Mum in the next room. She didn't know how it seemed to Dave, but to her it was just another milestone in the dull monotony of those years. Dave looking strange in a uniform, Mum lying paralysed in the next room, air-raid warnings – and a vague wish that she'd never been born. Dave left behind a package for her. A gramophone record, a watch, a pair of stockings and a note saying how much he'd enjoyed being with her. Nothing about love. She wondered if he meant the words on the record – "That Lovely Weekend".

She could remember the date of Alamein even now. It was October 23rd, 1942. She remembered it because that was the day Mum died. Neighbours rallied round and helped her to deal with all the formalities. She got a job straight away at her old place – in the offices of the foundry.

They were making shell cases then, not cookers and baths like in peace-time. It was a strange feeling being back with people again. A bit like prisoners must feel when they come out of jail or a nun who leaves a convent. She made a few friends. Went to the cinema once a week. She never went dancing. Not for any particular reason. She just didn't.

She had no idea where Dave was until almost the end of the war and she heard him singing on the radio in a Forces variety show. It seemed like somebody from another world. The real world maybe, not her monotonous one. She did have some regrets. She wished that she'd had the chance to tell him that she hadn't abandoned him. It was just that she couldn't abandon Mum either. She just wasn't any good at expressing what she felt. And she hadn't even known how to contact him.

She'd known Frank from when she first worked at the foundry as a wages clerk and they'd gone out regularly after Mum had died and she went back to work. She saw a piece in the *Daily Express* saying that Dave had married an Italian girl, and when Frank asked her to marry him she said yes. He'd been married before but his wife had been killed in an air-raid. He had two small children. A boy and a girl, and they all got on very well together. She supposed they were all getting what they wanted – more or less. She wouldn't say that she was wildly happy, but she was certainly not unhappy. She mattered to them, and that was enough. But she still wished that just once she'd had the chance to tell Dave how she'd really felt. That she'd loved him and hadn't abandoned him. She hadn't known how to explain it to him then. In those days it was the songs that said what you wanted to say yourself. She smiled to herself. Nobody'd ever written a song about choosing between a dying old lady and a man you loved.

The phone rang several times before she heard it, and she picked up the receiver without thinking.

'Hello.'

'It's Dave, Mary. How are you?'

For several moments she couldn't speak and then said in a whisper, 'Dave. How did you know my number?'

He laughed. 'I rang the foundry office – they told me. Anyway – how are you?'

'I'm fine.'

'And the family?'

'They're fine too. You've got a daughter, haven't you?'

'Yes. She's at drama school now.'

'And your wife?'

'Gabriella? Oh, she's fine – misses the Italian sun, of course.'

'Yes. We've not been having good weather down here.'

There was a long pause and then he said, 'Well I'm glad to hear that all's going well for you.'

'Yes. I'm fine – it was good of you to ring.'

Hesitantly he said, 'I'll say cheerio then – take care.'

'And you. 'Bye.' She slowly hung up the phone and whispered, 'Why, oh why didn't I tell him?'

I've written quite a lot of plays for BBC radio. I like radio and I liked the people in Radio Drama. They let me write about things other than espionage.

I wrote a play called "Music of a Small Life" *which marked out the life of an ordinary working man with the tunes that mattered to him at various times. I have always felt that hearing a song from the past brought back those days more vividly than words or pictures can do. The public seemed to respond well to that play and the BBC asked me to write a similar play but with a woman as a central character. It was called* "There's Always Tomorrow" *and this short story is based on that play.* Woman and Home *published it first, in early 1990.*

BOX NUMBER 742

When our switchboard girl said that a Mr Hacker wanted to speak to me I didn't recognise the name and, because I was in a meeting, I asked her to check who he was and what he wanted.

The meeting dragged on and she didn't come back to me, and for some reason I didn't notice the message she had left on my desk until the following morning. It said briefly: "Mr Hacker's call was personal. Knew you in Army. Will call again today. Angie."

I ought to have remembered his name even after ten years, but somehow when they give you your chalkstriped suit and your brown trilby and your accumulated pay it all kind of fades away. But you've signed a piece of paper that goes on about the Official Secrets Act and they side-line Clause 2. They also require you to keep them informed of any change of address.

I'd changed addresses three times since I was demobbed in 1947 and I hadn't notified them of any of the changes. Maybe subconsciously it was bloody-minded and deliberate, but there's enough to remember when you're moving home without worrying about keeping MI6 informed that you've moved from Finchley to Sanderstead.

When Hacker called mid-morning his voice was friendly and persuasive. They'd like to have a word with me. It was urgent and they'd like to suggest that we met at the Grosvenor Hotel at Victoria that afternoon. And that, as Hacker pointed out, was handy for my office and handy for catching my normal 5.17 from platform 16 at Victoria Station. I took the point silently that they knew my habits, and said I'd see them at four for tea and toast.

The agency was doing a pitch for the Cunard account in two days' time and the pressures meant that I thought no more about Hacker for the rest of the morning. But my efficient secretary sent me off to my rendezvous in good time.

The lounge of the Grosvenor Hotel still has a touch of Somerset Maugham about it. Men with distinguished white hair and heavy tans signal to waiters for more hot water with gestures that are distinctly east of Suez. Although Suez was not a word to be bandied about in those summer days of 1957.

They arrived on the dot at four. Hacker and Loveridge. It was like old times except that in those days it had tended to be whisky rather than tea.

Loveridge looked much the same. Shaggy and unkempt despite what were obviously expensive clothes. And his hair still looked as if it had been hacked at by the regimental barber. He still wore the heavy spectacles that emphasised the moon shape of his pale face. Nevertheless Arthur Loveridge could speak most Middle East languages better than the natives. The sad thing is that if you speak a foreign language perfectly you can seldom be used in the field because you stick out like a cat at Crufts against the rough demotic chat of the locals. So Loveridge was a desk man.

Hacker, like me, was somewhere in his middle thirties, and a field officer. We had both specialised in penetrating enemy underground movements. Hacker in what was then Persia and Iraq, and me against the Italians from east to north Africa and eventually in Italy. We were both successful operators but our masters had never been happy with our methods. We got criticised like the Met are criticised now, for hob-nobbing with the enemy. It was a waste of time explaining the facts of life to desk-bound majors in St James's Street. We might have been fighting to the death with a ruthless enemy, but there were things that a British officer could never do. Unfortunately Hacker and I did them, so I never made more than major and Hacker had to wait until I was demobbed before he got his turn. But it's an ill-wind, and Intelligence Corps pips and crowns with their green felt backing were in short supply and I was able to sell Joe Hacker my battle-dress jacket complete with crowns. One of the main differences between us was that Hacker loved parachuting, and I hated it. Somebody in Personnel once said to me that it was a very revealing characteristic on Hacker's part. I always reckoned it had something to do with the fact that Hacker wasn't very good with girls. He was good-looking and jolly but somehow he never clicked. There was something about Joe Hacker that girls rumbled. I still don't know what it was. I asked a girl once and she looked back half-smiling and shook her head. She had a knowing look in her eyes that implied that she knew something, all right, but didn't want to disillusion me.

We went through the usual bits about health and wives while the waiter was setting out the tea-things, and then Hacker leaned forward and tapped my knee.

'We need a bit of help, Johnny.'

'Go on.'

'You've read about the troubles in Cyprus?'

'You mean Makarios and all those acronyms – EOKA, ELAS, *Enosis*, and back to the Greek homeland stuff?'

'That's it.'

'I've never been to Cyprus, Joe. How can I help?'

'All the Greeks and Cypriots in this country have been sending out floods of cash for arms to murder our chaps who are trying to keep them from one another's throats. We've stopped all the individual money by Bank of England regulations, but the bastards have found one last dodge that we haven't been able to stop. That's where you could help.'

'Tell me.'

'They've bought up a small advertising agency and they ship the money out as payments for advertising in Cypriot newspapers. The ads never appear, of course, and the cash goes for buying arms.'

'And you want to stop it?'

'Yes.'

'Is it a genuine agency?'

'Yes. No big accounts, but it's legitimate, all right.'

'Has it got recognition?'

'What's that?'

'Is it recognised by the Institute? It can't place ads in the UK and get proper terms for discounts without recognition.'

Hacker looked at Loveridge with raised eyebrows and Loveridge, as always, knew the answer.

'Yes, it's fully recognised.'

'What sort of turnover?'

'About six hundred thousand, but a lot more if you throw in the cash going through to Cyprus.'

'How much more?'

'Twenty thousand a month more. Sometimes as much as forty.'

'Who subscribes it?'

'Every Greek and Cypriot waiter and ponce in Soho, for a start.'

'In cash?'

'Yes.'

I looked at Joe Hacker. 'Why don't you just send the boys in to wreck the place? They'll take the hint.'

'They'll just find some other dodge. Apart from that, the Foreign Office insists that we don't do anything that could be even vaguely made to look like harassment. We're still holding hands with Athens to try and cool it down.'

'Does this cash make any real difference?'

'It makes a lot of difference. It's about half of what they get from all sources.'

'What do you want me to do?'

'We want you to come up with some idea that stops this bloody agency playing games, without it being connected in any way with the Foreign Office or the security services.'

'Any ideas?'

'None. That's why we're talking to you.'

'How long have we got?'

'We want to clobber them as quickly as possible. A couple of months at the outside.'

'OK. I'll phone you tomorrow.'

We spent about fifteen minutes gossiping about our old friends and what they were doing in civilian life. The nice guys were on the bread-line teaching in secondary schools, and the real bastards had Ferraris and Rolls-Royces, living high off immoral earnings, or running arms and drugs in fast boats across the Med.

By the time I'd got to Sanderstead I had the first glimmerings of a possible way of dealing with our advertising friends. I slept on it and it still looked a runner next morning, but it had some holes in it.

Barnes Advertising Agency Limited was in Lower Belgrave Street and had been established for ten years. The two directors had sold out a year ago but had been kept on to run the place – the legitimate part, that is. They probably didn't even know about the fun and games that the new owners were up to.

There were four directors. The two original owners, both English: George Parker and Arthur Matins. And the two new owners: Panayotis Pattakos and Nicolas Sinodynos. At least those were the names on the registration at Companies House.

I phoned Hacker and arranged another meeting at the Grosvenor. Both of them came, and Hacker was obviously pleased that I had come back so quickly.

'What resources have we got, Joe?'

'What do you mean – money or people?'

'Both.'

'Very little money and no people. Are you expecting to make anything out of it?'

'Yes.'

His eyes were amused, and beady, and envious.

'How much?'

'Not money, just a favour.'

'Go on.'

'Get my agency one of the government advertising accounts. The Army recruiting campaign or short-service commissions. Something like that.'

'I haven't got that much influence.'

'I know. But your bosses have.'

He didn't like the dig but he nodded.

'I'll see what I can do.'

'Have you got any contacts in Tangier?'

'We've got an office there.'

'Any bods?'

'One from London and two locals.'

'Reliable?'

'Enough.'

'Who's in charge of Photographic now?'

'It's still Hamish McKay.'

'Can I borrow him?'

'How long for?'

'A couple of days.'

'That would be OK.'

'What's the money budget?'

He half-smiled. 'Tell me what you need.'

'About a thousand quid. Maybe you'll get some change or maybe I'll need a bit more.'

'What's the plan?'

'You'd best not know, sweetheart. Just leave it to me.'

'If we're going to be involved I want to know what's going on.'

'Just tell McKay that I can use him. Hand over the cash and you won't hear any more.'

'How long will it take?'

'Three to four weeks.'

'What do you want, pounds or dollars?'

'Doesn't matter. Whatever's easier.'

'I'll send you the cash tomorrow morning. But I'll want a receipt and I'll want an accounting when it's all over.'

I tried not to smile as I thought of the accounting.

'That's OK, Joe. Send it to me at the office.'

It had taken Hamish McKay just over two days but I'm sure it wasn't longer than necessary or because he enjoyed it. I enjoyed it, but I was more or less an observer.

I saw the ad in *Advertisers' Weekly* the following Friday. It was in the classified section. Brief and innocent:

Moroccan tours company seeks small/medium-sized advertising agency to handle small account £20/30,000. Box No 742, Advertiser's Weekly, Mercury House, London SW2.

I spent two days organising things in Tangier the next weekend. We had had twenty-three responses to the ad, and I sent a cable to Barnes Advertising confirming that they had the account and asking them to phone their acceptance. They phoned the same evening and I did my Marseilles accent, read them out the copy and told them to put four-inch doubles in the *Church Times*, the *Catholic Herald* and the *Jewish Chronicle*. I don't believe in either favouritism or prejudice.

I got Hacker to give me a list of twenty-five names and addresses and told him what I wanted done by the Post Office Special Unit.

It took two weeks before there was enough material and I phoned Hacker for another meeting. I said it had to be in private and opted for my office.

He sat the other side of my desk opening the envelopes one by one. It took him quite a time and then he looked across at me.

'D'you mean to say Hamish McKay did these?'

'Under my direction he did.'

'Not in the studio at Broadway, surely?'

'No, we hired one.'

'And the girls?'

'We hired them, too.'

'I don't want that on the account sheet.'

'We just put it down as models.'

'Not bloody likely we don't.'

'OK, we just bump up the hire-charge for the studio.'

'I don't want to know, mate. It's all yours. What happens next?'

'Just leave it to me. I'll contact you. But I want a telephone number manned round the clock.'

'That's no problem.'

'When it rings, they say "Post Office Legal Department". They'll ask for Mr Harris. That's me. I'm not there but I'm expected back. Take their number and I'll call them back. Let me know as soon as they call. Here or at home. Answer no questions. Absolutely nothing. OK?'

'OK,' he said reluctantly.

'D'you want a drink?'

'A whisky if you've got one.'

I went into the outer office and got the glasses and the bottle. We were there about another hour. After he had gone I piled up the envelopes and sorted the sheep from the goats. The goats were the ones on my list of names and addresses from Hacker. It took me over an hour because there were two empty envelopes. I went over my desk, the carpet, then the whole of my office but the envelopes stayed empty.

I spent two hours the next morning at the Chambers of one of SIS's barrister advisers. He was obviously mystified by my interest in that particular section of the law but he ploughed through it as I made notes.

I pressed the brass bell at the side of the bright blue door and it buzzed and opened. In the small foyer was an old dear at a desk with a small switchboard. I asked for Mr Pattakos.

'He's not here, I'm afraid.'

'Is Mr Parker in?'

'Yes, but he's very busy.'

'I'd like to see him.'

'What name shall I say?'

'Harris. Mr Harris.'

She mumbled into the telephone and then hung up.

'If you'll take a seat, he'll see you in a few minutes. He only sees space reps by appointment, you know.'

Parker came down about ten minutes later. He was in his late fifties. White hair. He could have been used by Central Casting for any "English gentleman" part. He could have played Andy Hardy's father without a touch of make-up.

'Mr Hollis, is it?' he said.

'Harris. James Harris.'

'I haven't got more than a couple of minutes, I'm afraid.'

'Could I see you in private?'

He looked surprised. 'Is that necessary?'

'I think it would be better.'

When he hesitated I said very softly, 'I've got a warrant for your arrest.'

I followed him slowly up the narrow stairs and into a pleasant modern office. He waved limply towards one of the chairs round the table and sat down himself. He looked tense but not scared as he pushed a couple of files to one side.

'Now,' he said. 'I suppose this is some sort of mistake?'

'You're George Hamilton Parker, a director of the Barnes Advertising Agency Limited, yes?'

'Yes.'

'And you placed advertising on behalf of Moroccan Enterprises?'

'Yes. They're a comparatively new client.'

'You looked into their background, of course?'

He frowned. 'No. They paid in advance and there's no way we could check on them; they're based in Morocco.'

'You didn't check with our embassy or the Board of Trade?'

'No.'

'Did you check on their product?'

'There isn't a product. They offer a week's holiday in Tangier.'

'You checked the airline and the accommodation?'

'No. The airline's British charter and we assumed the accommodation's all right.'

'D'you remember the copy in the ad?'

'No.'

I pulled out the ad and put it on the table and pointed to the coupon.

'It says, "Send for full details of the good time you'll get with Moroccan Enterprises".'

He nodded and looked at me, his eyebrows raised.

'Did you produce their reply?'

'No. They said they had brochures already and that it was better for enquirers to get the material direct from Tangier. People like a foreign post-mark and a stamp.'

'You mean you didn't even see what they were sending through the post?'

'No.'

'I can't believe that, Mr Parker.'

'I assure you it's true.'

I put the briefcase on the table and took out a bundle of the envelopes and pushed them across the table towards him.

'Have a look at those.'

His hands trembled as he picked up the first envelope and slid out the contents. There was the postcard and the original coupon from the ad.

He stared at the postcard then reached for another envelope and went through the same routine.

'They're all the same type of material, Mr Parker. Turn one over and read what's on the back.'

I saw his lips moving as he read the words. I knew them by heart because I'd written them. They weren't the best copy I'd ever written but they did the job. On the back of each postcard it said, "This is just part of the fun you get on a Moroccan Enterprise holiday in Tangier – sin city of North Africa."

He'd had time to read *War and Peace* before he put the card down and looked across at me.

'There's obviously been a terrible mistake. I'll have to look into it.'

'I'm afraid it's too late for that, Mr Parker. We have already looked into it. You've not only been grossly negligent but you've committed a whole heap of offences.'

'But we had no idea . . .'

'You'll be able to explain that to the court. Meantime, I've got warrants to serve on the four directors. Are they all here?'

'I'm afraid that Mr Makins is out.'

'Are the other two here?'

'Only Mr Pattakos.'

'Perhaps you could ask him to step down here and have a word with me?'

'I'll see if I can find him.'

'I'll come with you,' I said.

We went up two floors and the old boy knocked on the door marked "Private" and a voice with an accent called out, 'Come in'.

It was a large room that had probably once been an attic but it was now an office, living quarters and bedroom combined. It smelt faintly aromatic, or perhaps it was incense.

The young man sipping coffee in an armchair was good-looking but not handsome. More Greek than Cypriot with a light olive skin and soft spaniel eyes. There was nothing of the brigand about him. He sat with his coffee cup poised in front of his mouth as Parker introduced me. When he came to the bit about warrants for arrest, Pattakos slowly put down his cup and saucer on the coffee table. The brown eyes looked up at me and he said softly, 'May I see the warrant and your identity card?'

I put both on the table. He glanced at my ID but read the warrant carefully. He reached for the telephone without looking and dragged it in front of him. He dialled a number and waited, and lit a cigarette before he spoke.

'*Pyos, ine eki? . . . moo thinete ton Kirio Papadopolos, parakalo . . .*'

The conversation went on for six or seven minutes and he looked at me intently while he was talking. When he hung up he said, 'My lawyer says that all you can do is confiscate the material.'

'That only applies to the charge under the Customs Consolidation Act 1876. The main charges, as you can see, are under the Post Office Act 1953, Section Eleven.'

'We were deceived for some reason.'

'You were negligent not to check what your clients were doing.'

'The Act specifies "for gain". We made no gain.'

'The Act states the gain may accrue indirectly. Your gain was commission from the journals for placing the ads.'

He gave me a long searching look. 'Can I see the material?'

I gave him half a dozen envelopes and he looked at them and their contents slowly and carefully. Eventually he looked at Parker and said, 'Leave it to me, George. I'll see you later.'

When Parker had left, Pattakos leaned back in his chair and lit another cigarette. He closed his eyes as he inhaled and when he opened them he leaned forward towards me.

'You'd better go down the list.'

'What list?'

'The penalties you've got in mind.'

'You've seen the charges.'

'I'm talking about the penalties.'

'It's up to three years' imprisonment for each of you, plus fines.'

'And we lose our agency recognition and have to close down?'

'I should think so.'

He nodded slowly. 'My lawyer advises me that there is a defence of "no reasonable cause to suspect" what was going on.'

'That would probably work for an individual but not for a company. Negligence isn't a defence.'

He loosened his tie and lit another cigarette. His brown eyes were neither angry nor disturbed.

'What is it you're after?'

'I'm just serving the warrants.'

He tapped the ash from his cigarette into the ashtray, still looking at me. 'I'd go up to twenty thousand in sterling or dollars, your choice.'

'You're just getting in deeper, Mr Pattakos. The penalties for bribery are just as heavy.'

'What is it you want?'

'I don't want anything and I advise . . .'

'What do your people want?'

'You mean the Director of Public Prosecutions?'

He shook his head. 'No. I mean that I know we've been framed and I want to know what it's going to cost.'

'What have you got in mind?'

He stared at me for a few moments. 'I'm a politician, not a crook. I'll do whatever is necessary. I don't give a damn about going to prison, that would get me more votes in the next elections than I could hope for now. But it wastes my time, and the organisation needs me right now.'

'So?'

'I could close down the agency.'

'Do the two old boys know what you were up to?'

'No. Of course not.'

'Would you pay them pensions or compensation?'

'No. They were paid a fair price for the agency.'

'I'd better mention that your bank accounts have been frozen.'

'Since when?'

'Since nine o'clock this morning. We've found six but we'll freeze any others we find. Personal as well as business.'

For the first time the brown eyes looked angry. He opened his mouth to speak but lit another cigarette instead.

'OK,' he said. 'What do you want?'

'You close the agency. You don't try and sell it. You give the two old boys a lump sum each of ten thousand. And that's the end of it.'

'What do we get?'

'You don't go to jail. You don't pay fines. You and your partner leave the country within fourteen days. You don't try playing games through the Greek Embassy to stay.'

'How long have I got to decide?'

'A couple of minutes.'

He stubbed out an almost whole cigarette and lit another. As he put down the lighter he said, 'OK. It's a deal.'

I stayed around until he'd put his part in train and then headed for Hacker's office.

His girl said he'd be back by four so I waited. And for some unknown reason I thought of the missing postcards. At Matlock they'd said, 'If you've only got two minutes in an office, always go for the bottom right-hand drawer.'

And there they were, under a copy of the *Spectator*, both of them face down. I turned them face up and I suddenly understood why Hacker didn't get on with girls. They were both of the young blonde who called herself Michelle and was more likely a Maisie from Birmingham. She was about twenty and very pretty. They were the only two shots we had taken of that particular type and I'd had to phone one of SIS's tame psychiatrists to find out what they did. She was well-built and the ropes cut into her firm young breasts and across her belly and her thighs. That was the least abnormal part of the pose and for the rest you'd have to dislike girls an awful lot to get any kind of kick out of doing it or seeing it.

I closed the drawer and left a note on Hacker's desk.

The small agency went out of business ten days later and in about 1960 I saw a picture of Pattakos in *The Times*. He was standing a couple of places from Archbishop Makarios, who was waving to his fans from a balcony in Athens.

This was the first short story I ever wrote, for Winter's Crimes 12 *edited by Hilary Watson in 1980, and re-reading it, it all seems a long time ago. Back to the days when I worked at an advertising agency and had a telephone call not dissimilar to the one I've described. In those early days my mind went more to plots rather than characters. If I were writing this story today it would be much longer and the characters more solid. In the writing game you have to learn as you go along.*

THE WALKING WOUNDED

Karol Zeromski sat on his small bed, taking off his boots and whistling "Waltzing in the Clouds". He had been in love with Deanna Durbin for nearly a year. He had written her a letter two months ago, asking for a signed photograph. There had been no reply as yet but he understood that. Maybe she didn't speak Polish.

He put on his slippers and walked to the door of the room he shared with his two brothers and listened. They were still at it. Those old boys from the Judenrat arguing with his father about whether Hrubice was a *wieś* or a *miasto*. A village or a town. The old men of the Judenrat wanted Hrubice to be classified as a *miasto*. If Hrubice was a town they could demand higher payments from their fellow Jews and Karol's father was the wealthiest man in Hrubice. He was shouting that Hrubice was a village and always would be a village. If it was a town, where was the Town Hall? Where was the court and where was the jail?

Karol sighed and went back to sit on his bed. He had already finished his homework but he picked up his maths book again. He liked maths, especially algebra. Algebra was like a dream, or poetry. It didn't deal in *zlotys* and *kopeks*, or even oranges and lemons. It never said what "a" or "b" was. They could be anything. Swans or fairy princesses with long blonde hair like his sister Halinka.

An hour later he was asleep.

They were in the middle of the geography lesson when the headmaster came into the classroom, obviously agitated as he

157

whispered to old Jaworski before rushing out again, jacket tails flying.

Jaworski held up his hand for silence, then wiped his moustache with the back of his hand. And there was a murmur from the class when they saw that Jaworski had tears running down his cheeks.

'There is terrible news, boys. In the middle of the night the Germans invaded our dear Poland. Our gallant soldiers are resisting the treacherous attack with all their resources and courage. The school is closed until further notice. You must all return to your homes.'

For a few moments after Jaworski left the room there was silence and then a hubbub of excited voices. No school. Maybe no school for as long as a week until the cavalry shoved the Germans back where they belonged. There had been talk for years about the Germans demanding a corridor to Danzig, but there was always somebody demanding a change in frontiers or Ukrainians claiming lost territory. Headlines in the paper for a few days and then it all faded away.

There was a family meeting that night. Uncles, aunts and cousins and Grandma Zeromski. Uncle Feliks was the one they listened to. He'd heard on the radio that the Germans were using tanks against the cavalry, and dive-bombers were attacking the towns that lay between the frontier and Warsaw. But Hrubice was only twenty kilometres from the Russian border and the Germans wouldn't risk tangling with the Russkis. They should stay where they are and see what happened. And everyone agreed. There was no need to panic.

But when the others had left, Grandma Zeromski had taken Karol and his father into the kitchen, alone.

'Look at this boy, Jacek. Your son. Blond hair, blue eyes, he could be one of those Germans. Look at his face. No sign there of being a Jew. You understand, Jacek?'

'No, Babcia.'

'Whatever Feliks says, the Germans will come. Russians or no Russians. He has a chance. You've got to give him that chance, Jacek.'

'I don't understand.'

'You send him away. Where he is not known. From now on he is a Catholic. Maybe then he is not only saved himself but he can help the rest of us too.'

The father looked at his son. 'What do you think, son?'

'I'll do whatever you say, Father. But why does it matter if I'm a Jew?'

'The Poles are bad enough about us Jews, boy. But the Germans are much worse. They brought in laws to exterminate the Jews. They are killing even German Jews. They will be worse when they get here.'

'Where shall I go?'

'I have a friend who is a Catholic in a small town on the River Bug. He owes me many favours and he's a kind, good man. He will look after you.'

'How far away is it?'

'Not far. About forty kilometres. I'll get in touch with him tomorrow. Mama will put some things together for you to take with you.'

On the following Sunday Jacek had hired a horse and cart and they had driven through the night to Uscilug to the house of Jacek's friend, Tomasz Jodlowski.

Jodlowski was an engineer. A man much older than his father. He was a silent, withdrawn man, but kind, and he looked after the fifteen-year-old boy as best he could, being careful to carry out his friend's wishes by taking the boy to church every Sunday.

Tomasz Jodlowski had a short-wave radio which he listened to each night in the attic, and sometimes he let Karol listen with him. They heard of the fall of Norway and then of Belgium and Holland. And, later, the incredible news of the Germans marching into Paris. There was a platoon of German Wehrmacht billeted in the town but they were not aggressive and people went about their business in the normal way. Karol was working as an assistant to Tomasz Jodlowski who was supervising the building of a carpet factory. It began to look as if Grandma Zeromski's fears had been groundless. But on the night of June 21st, 1941, the unbelievable happened. The Germans invaded Russia.

In a matter of days the whole border area became a maelstrom of Wehrmacht troops. The Luftwaffe bombers droned over continuously and by the end of the first week there were tens of thousands of Russian prisoners being housed in makeshift open-air camps. And in Russia itself the Red Army was fleeing in total disorder.

And now, every town and village was under full control of the Germans and there were rumours of special units called

Einsatzkommandos whose task was to seek out and kill every Jew, man, woman and child, that they could find.

A message came through that Karol's family had fled to the woods and were constantly moving to escape the Germans. As he lay in bed that night Karol couldn't sleep. His imagination could not encompass the thought of his father and mother, brothers and sister living out in the woods. And even Grandma Zeromski. Leaving their comfortable house, their beds, their possessions. He found himself shivering. Not from cold but from fear. He had asked Pan Jodlowski if he ought to go and join them. But Jodlowski had said that he was to do what his parents wanted and stay with him.

A week later Jodlowski had sent him to the far side of the town for a set of drawing compasses and on his way back he saw a crowd gathered by the railway station. He asked a man what was happening and he was told that the people filing into the station were the Jews. All Jews had to report that day to the station to go to a work-camp. Karol watched the columns of frightened men, women and children waiting their turn to be loaded on the waggons with SS-men shouting orders, beating those who got out of line with the butts of rifles. There were babies in arms and crying toddlers being comforted by their parents. He heard a man near him shout out 'Dirty Jews' and he hurried away. He couldn't bear the sight of those ordinary people being treated like cattle. His throat was dry and he wanted to scream.

He went into the church on his way back and prayed to a God he didn't believe in. Prayed for his family and prayed for himself. Prayed for courage, and prayed for forgiveness for his blasphemy and cowardice.

In the next few weeks the news from the BBC said that the Russians were holding out and the German Army was falling back. The Russian winter was taking a vicious toll of the German soldiers. And each day now there were carts and waggons full of frostbitten Germans trundling through the town, day and night. But the German retreat only seemed to enrage the local German troops to further persecution of the Jews. And now they were using Ukrainian deserters as guards and exterminators. A Jew only had to appear on the streets and he would be shot.

Not long after Christmas a message came through from Hrubice that all the family had been shot in a sudden round-up of all Jews by an Einsatzkommando. People were too scared now to give Jews even a night's hiding place.

Two weeks later one of the Einsatzkommandos blocked off both ends of the street where Jodlowski lived and had his workshop and office. Jodlowski had sent Karol up to the attic and told him to stay there. He could hear the Germans shouting '*Juden raus*' and there were shots and machine-gun fire.

He heard the outer door being battered open, then the clatter of heavy boots and shouts in German. A Ukrainian guard was asking where Jodlowski was hiding the Jews. Jodlowski said there were no Jews on the premises and then there were other voices and the ladder to the attic was shaking and, seconds later, an SS-man with the dreaded Death's Head badge was staring at Karol. He had a pistol in his hand and he beckoned Karol to come down the ladder.

In the room below there were three SS-men and a Ukrainian and the man who had come up the ladder waved his gun at Karol, shouting to him to let down his trousers and pull up his shirt. When they saw that he had been circumcised the SS-man swore at Jodlowski as he raised his gun. The bullets smashed into Jodlowski's face and chest, sending him reeling backwards against the wall before he slid slowly to the concrete floor. Even when he was obviously dead the SS-man fired two more bullets into the inert body.

They tore the clothes from Karol and shoved him naked into the street. There were thirty or more naked Jews huddled together, men and women and two children. Then, with the guards shouting orders, the group were marched down the street and a woman in an upstairs window lifted a child to watch the sorry procession shambling along in silence, many of them familiar neighbours.

They were driven like cattle up a side-street to what had once been a public park and was now used for growing potatoes, and Karol saw more groups of naked Jews. And then as they neared the other groups Karol saw to his horror that they were standing in rough lines on the edge of a freshly dug pit. There was a strange, eerie silence that only emphasised the shouted commands of the SS-men. As Karol was pushed into line he saw the rifles being raised. And then the shots and screams as bodies collapsed and fell into the pit. A man held Karol's hand as they were pushed forward by the guards and the man spoke from the corner of his mouth. 'When we are in the front, fall into the ditch as soon as they fire the first shot. Don't jump, just fall and stay quite still.'

Karol could hear women wailing and a man intoning a prayer in Yiddish and then they were on the edge of the pit. As the first

161

shot sounded he felt a hard blow in his back that unbalanced him and he fell forward, dropping ten feet on to the heaped piles of naked corpses. He was barely conscious of the continuous firing and bodies flying through the air, and slowly he lost consciousness altogether, oblivious to the screams and the bodies piling up around him.

He came to gasping against the stench of dead bodies and the smell of fresh earth, and found he could move his head and one arm. He pushed his arm up slowly and struggled against the weight of the soil until he was kneeling, his back arched, both hands grabbing at the loose earth that covered him. Slowly he raised his body, crouching on all-fours, straightening his back and then, raising his head, he could feel cold air on his upstretched arms. He summoned up the last of his strength, pushing the earth aside until his head was above the soil. It was dark but there was a full moon behind the slow-moving clouds. It took another half hour to free his body and when he stood on the damp grass he closed his eyes against the stick-like arms and legs rising stiffly from the surface of the pit.

He sat with his head in his hands, his body shaking in an ague of fear, his mind utterly confused. He had escaped death in the pit, but for what good? He was naked, with nowhere to go and nobody who would give him shelter. The people's fear of the SS was total. There was no room for Good Samaritans. He stumbled to the main street which was silent and empty, and animal instinct led him to the house where he had lived. The door was hanging by one iron hinge and, inside, Jodlowski's body still lay there but every stick of furniture had gone. Everything, even the kitchen utensils and the food that had been ready for them to eat.

Slowly, his hands trembling, he worked the clothes off Jodlowski's stiff body. His shirt, his trousers, his jacket and his big boots. He dressed in them slowly and they felt almost too heavy for his body to support.

As he stood leaning against the frame of the street door he heard the church clock strike just once. And as if it were a signal he walked down the cobbled street to the church. When he got there the door was ajar and he walked unsteadily inside. He saw three candles burning by the altar, their flames flickering in the breeze from the open door. He fell to his knees, his head resting on the back of the seat in front of him, his face in his hands. He wanted to pray but he couldn't think what he wanted to pray for.

It was almost ten minutes later when the priest stood in front of the young man, waiting for him to stand up or raise his head. But he did neither and then the priest reached out and put his hand gently on the blond head. When Karol looked up at the priest's face the priest said quietly, 'Come with me.' Karol tried hard to struggle to his feet but failed, and the priest lifted him up and, with his arm around his shoulder, half-carried, half-dragged the young man to the sacristy, taking one of the lighted candles as he passed.

As Karol lay with his eyes closed on the small truckle-bed the priest eased off the ill-fitting clothes and then slowly and gently washed the grime from the young man's body. Finally, he gave him a sip of brandy and as his patient seemed to be recovering, he left the room for a few moments. When he came back he brought clothing that was more Karol's size and when the young man was dressed the priest hung a medallion around his neck.

'That, my son, is a holy medal – *Matka Boska Częstochowska* – the Holy Mother of God of Częstochowa. People sometimes call it The Black Madonna – *Czarna Madona*. May it keep you safe at all times. Pray to her every day and when you are in danger.'

Karol nodded. 'Thank you, Father.'

It was the loud voices and the sunlight streaming through the window that roused him. He could hear the priest talking in German and a rough voice shouting him down. Then they were in the room. There were two of them with the priest, an SS-man and a Ukrainian militia-man. The SS-man was pointing at Karol.

'That's the one. The old woman saw him creeping in here in the dark.'

'The boy is a Catholic, my friend, not a Jew.'

'Then let him prove it, let him take down his trousers.'

The priest smiled. 'That proves nothing. That's a question of hygiene, not race or religion.'

'I don't believe that.'

The priest smiled. 'Do you think I might be a secret Jew, soldier?'

'No, Father.'

'Well, I am like that, too.'

'So this fellow can argue all that at the labour-camp. He's got to go. It's orders. If he isn't a Jew then he's a vagrant. It's all the same.'

'Where will he go?'

'With the others to Birkenau.'

163

'Is that the camp at Auschwitz?'

'That's it.'

The SS-man turned to Karol. 'Get your belongings into a small bag.'

'I don't have any belongings.'

He had been taken with thirty-five other prisoners on an open lorry to the camp where he had been issued the striped prisoners' jacket and trousers. The black triangles on his right trouser leg and his jacket marked him as the category "anti-social", but there was no superimposed yellow triangle that would make up the Star of David and mark him as a Jew. He was marched to one of the blocks in the men's camp known as BIIc.

The block was crammed with three-tier wooden bunks; there had been no place that night for him and he had slept on a concrete floor in a mire of human excrement.

The next day he had seen a hundred or more old men and women and young children being marched past the block to the far side of the camp. Another prisoner had told him they were headed for the gas-chamber. Gas-chamber IV had been prepared for them overnight. When he asked what they had done the man said they had done nothing, but neither old people nor children could work and were always sent to the gas-chamber and crematorium within a few days of arrival.

Slowly he learned the meaning of the different coloured triangles on their striped uniforms. Brown for gypsies, green for criminals, mauve for Jehovah's Witnesses, pink for homosexuals, red for politicals, and the most common, yellow, for Jews.

In the next few weeks Karol Zeromski learned that survival came only from a ruthless selfishness that squandered no pity or remorse on seeing his fellows brutally treated, killed or tortured by guards who took open pleasure in inflicting pain and humiliation on their helpless captives. Men who killed for trivial reasons or no reason at all. What shocked him most was the *kapos*. Prisoners who were put in authority over other prisoners. Men who were as sadistic as the SS guards themselves. When he discovered that there were Jewish *kapos* who treated the Jewish prisoners with an uncontrolled fury that was even more ruthless than that of the German guards, he found it hard to imagine how such men could have become like savages. Laughing and shouting obscenities as they clubbed a man to death.

He was given work as a painter and that gave him chances to

steal food, and drugs for his almost continuous dysentery. There were Russians, Germans, Yugoslavs, Hungarians and many Poles in the camp, but Karol Zeromski learned that you could expect no more help or mercy from your own countrymen than from any others. Survival was all. It was loners who survived.

Despite the nightmare existence, his dreams were of food and clean clothes. His family were part of a past that he didn't believe had ever been.

The summer of 1985 was not a good summer but on that particular day the sun streamed through the windows of the hall and showed up motes of dust in the air. But it wasn't an occasion for noticing dust.

Colonel Lambton stood surrounded by fifty or so parishioners of the Church of Our Lady, all laughing and chattering until the colonel lifted his hand to silence them, smiling as he said, 'Well, my friends, there's only one person here who doesn't know what it's all about and that's my good friend – our good friend – Father Jerome.' He paused as he turned to the white-haired priest. 'Father, when you came to this church fifteen years ago, you came to a church that was in a poor state. Both the building and its souls sorely in need of sustenance. You – with your hard work and self-sacrifice – ever-calm, ever-caring – have put new life into a district that had been abandoned by politicians and local leaders alike.

'You know already of our love, affection and respect for you as both a priest and a man. Our children, our families, owe so much to you and your work and your ministry. Now . . .' he said smiling, '. . . behind that curtain – which usually covers nothing more exciting than the Women's Guild crockery and cooking utensils – we have something from all of us, to you.'

The colonel turned to a stout lady in a large hat and a veil. 'So, Mrs O'Hara, will you do the honours and pull back the curtain?'

The stout lady pulled back the curtain, which had been laundered specially for the occasion, to reveal the table from the sacristy with the black metal-cased equipment of a hi-fi rack-system with a pair of large speakers. And as the elderly priest stood looking at the equipment, the colonel pressed one of the switches and, seconds later, the music of Fauré's *Requiem* filled the rather sombre church-hall. They listened quietly for a few minutes and then the old colonel switched it off.

Father Jerome was obviously moved by his parishioners' affection but he had never been a man for flowery speeches and he said quietly, 'It was very kind of you all to think of me in this way. I shall enjoy using it.' He paused and took a deep breath, his voice catching as he said, 'This parish was my first love and my only love. Thank you all for your kindness to me. I only wish that I had deserved it.' He smiled briefly. 'May God bless you all.'

As they walked home together the colonel, who was also the only doctor in the run-down area, said to his wife, 'You know, the Church is very lucky to have men like him. Devoted to his ministry. Caring for those stupid wretches who have never learned how to live sensible lives.'

She laughed softly. 'And what about you, my boy? You could have had a nice middle-class practice in some pleasant suburb instead of this wretched place.'

'Couldn't face all those twin-sets and pearls, my dear.'

'You and he are very alike, you know. Not outwardly, but inside, you are.'

'Tell me more.'

'Outside you're different. You always smiling and him always looking so sad. But inside it's as if you've both seen all the frailty of us humans and still can find excuses, or reasons, for our sins and shortcomings. Maybe soldiers and priests are much the same. Just different uniforms.'

'I'd have to think about that, my dear. Sounds very profound.' He smiled. 'Anyway, I'm lucky, I've got you.'

She laughed and squeezed his arm. 'Well, he's got his lady, too.'

'So he has. So he has. To each his own.'

As the doctor put down his black bag he saw the message propped up on the hall-stand. It was scrawled in felt pen and at the top was printed the word "URGENT". The message itself said that somebody had phoned to say that Father Jerome was sick and please go to see him. It was signed "Olive". Olive was the cleaning lady.

He got the Fiesta out of the garage again and headed off for the church.

Doctor Lambton folded up his stethoscope slowly and repacked his bag to give himself time to think before he turned back to look at the frail man on the bed. They all called him elderly but he was only a few months past his sixtieth birthday. He just seemed older. Much older. Father Jerome was wearing just a shirt that Lambton had had to open to apply the stethoscope. He was shocked by the thin frame, the ribs all clearly visible, the skin the colour of uncooked pastry.

He made himself more comfortable on the edge of the bed and looked at his patient.

'How long since you had a holiday or a break, Father?'

'I don't need holidays or breaks, George.'

'How long? And I want an answer.'

'Why does it matter?'

'When did you get pneumonia?'

'A long time ago. When I was a kid.'

'What did you take for it?'

'It was war-time, George. It just slowly got better.'

'I've got news for you, my friend. It left two damn great scars. One on each lung. You must have had difficulty breathing all your life.'

'Sometimes. But I get by. Is anything else the matter?'

'Tell me again what happened.'

'Mrs Painter had been arranging the flowers in the church for tomorrow and I was telling her how nice they looked and I kind of blacked-out. Fainted or something. She and old Foster got me into bed.' He shrugged. 'And here I am. Waiting for the bad news.'

'Apart from what I told you about your lungs there is no bad news. Not physical bad news, anyway.'

'So?'

'The reason why you blacked out was because you're worn-out, exhausted. You don't eat enough, you don't get enough rest and you need your batteries re-charging.' He paused. 'I'm going to give your housekeeper some menus and you've got to follow them or you'll be in my bad books. Understood?'

Father Jerome smiled wanly. 'Yes. Thanks for caring about me.'

'You old fool. The whole parish cares about you.'

'I don't deserve it.'

'Rubbish.'

Patsy Lambton switched off the radio in the kitchen as her husband came in.

'Just in time, the tea's brewing.' She looked at his face, anxious. 'How was he?'

Lambton walked through to the hall and got rid of his bag and then, back in the kitchen, he sat at the kitchen table as his wife poured the tea.

'So how was he, George?'

'Frankly, I don't know.'

'What's that mean?'

'He's got patches on his lungs. Says they're from when he was young.' He pursed his lips. 'God knows why his parents didn't get him proper treatment. Said it was war-time but, war or no war, he needed proper medical treatment. It leaves him short of breath which is why he probably doesn't talk much.'

'So what's worrying you?'

'I don't rightly know. But there's something wrong there, that's for sure.'

'Like what?'

Dr Lambton took a deep breath, then let it out slowly before looking at his wife as he said softly, 'If we weren't talking about a priest I'd suspect either drugs or some kind of mental problem.'

'You mean drug abuse?'

'Yes.'

'Why do you think this?'

'Instinct maybe. And experience. He's a sick man but, except for the lungs and the gross underweight, there's nothing physically wrong.' He sighed. 'Maybe a rest and a change of scene would put him right.' He smiled at her fondly. 'Needs a good wife.'

He was coming out of the hospital where he'd been visiting a patient with a new baby when the police car drew up and the driver waved to him. As he bent down at the car window the policeman said, 'Inspector Davis wants you to come with me to the church.'

'What's the matter?'

'He just told me to find you and bring you over.'

Ten minutes later they were at the church and the doctor hurried inside. He walked down the aisle and through to the priest's room. The police inspector was sitting beside the priest's bed and the doctor saw at once that the old priest was dead.

The inspector stood up and held out his hand. 'Inspector Davis. We met at my daughter's wedding.'

'I remember it well. What has happened?'

'I think he died in his sleep. The housekeeper found him at six a.m. and she phoned the station. I was just leaving but I came over myself.' The doctor was aware of an odd look in the policeman's eye. As if he were sending a different message with his eyes, or some kind of warning.

'There'll have to be an inquest.'

'That's why I wanted you here, so that you could check that his death appeared to be natural.'

Dr Lambton frowned. 'What do you mean, *appears* to be natural.'

'If, after your examination, you decide that it was death from natural causes – he was, after all, an old man – there would be no need for an autopsy unless the police felt there were suspicious circumstances – and we don't have any such suspicions.' He paused. 'I understand you were treating him.'

'Just a visit about six weeks ago. He'd had a black-out.'

'What caused the black-out?'

'One can't be sure. I put it down to age and overwork.'

'He left a note, addressed to you.'

'Where is it?'

The inspector reached into his jacket pocket and gave the doctor a sealed envelope. It had his name on in capital letters. Slowly he tore it open, folded back the single sheet of notepaper and read it.

Dear George,

Please forgive me. All of you. For I have deceived you. I am a Jew. I was in Auschwitz. I can no longer live with my memories. As you rightly said – I need a rest. There is no rest for me on earth.

Again, forgive me,

Karol Zeromski

(known as Father Charles Jerome)

The doctor folded the paper and put it into his pocket as he turned to the inspector.

'It was just a personal note.'

The inspector nodded. 'Will you check him over?'

Fifteen minutes later the doctor closed his bag and looked at the inspector. 'There are no signs of violence. Nothing suspicious. And I'll say so to the coroner.'

'He was a good man to the people around here.'

The doctor looked at the policeman's face. 'And this way, nobody gets hurt or disillusioned.'

Inspector Davis nodded and handed the bottle from his pocket to the doctor. 'The housekeeper never saw that. It was under his pillow.'

After the inspector had left the doctor wandered around the small room. There was a crucifix on one wall and a calendar from the local grocery shop. A plain bentwood chair beside the single bed, an old dressing-gown hanging on a hook on the back of the door. The hi-fi was on a small baize-covered card-table, with the speakers on a shelf over the blocked-up fireplace and a shoe-box that held a dozen or so cassettes.

Slowly he walked back to the bed and looked at the old priest's body. Gently he crossed the hands together on his chest and closed the staring, unseeing eyes. He looked briefly at the bottle that he still had in his hand. The label said it had held a hundred aspirins. There were three left in the bottom of the bottle. Sighing, he put it into his bag and then walked slowly to the door. And as he paused there he saw that the little red light indicated that the hi-fi was still on.

He walked over and switched it off and then noticed that the key was pressed to "Tape" and there was still a cassette left in the hi-fi. He pressed the eject button, took out the cassette and closed the machine. As he went to place the cassette with the others in the shoe-box he glanced at the title. The label said *Deanna Durbin Sings Again*.

My wife's mother, Czeslawa Felinska, was Polish and my wife was born in a Polish Army camp in North Wales, so I have a soft spot for the Poles. Treated with almost incredible brutality by both the Germans and the Russians, it is amazing that they have survived with such spirit and determination that they were the first of the Warsaw Pact countries to win back at least some basic freedom.

We are inextricably bound up with them. We were the only country who fought Hitler and the rest of them without waiting to be attacked ourselves. We declared war because the Nazis invaded Poland. We couldn't save them from defeat and when the war ended we shamefully left them to their fate. We were too worn out and the Russians and the Americans decided Europe's fate between them.

I had a letter a few months back from Solidarnosc's official publisher. They had found a copy of one of my books in the flea-market in Gdansk and had translated it. They asked for permission to publish it which I gladly gave.

GRACE AND FAVOUR

When you've just cleaned out the boat's bilges you expect a feeling of righteousness, but you don't expect a reward. But this was not one of those days. With my face level with the aft-deck I looked up at the jetty. They were the longest, shapeliest, sexiest legs I'd seen for many a day. And, as the French always say, they went right up to her bottom. They disappeared beneath a short white skirt which flowed from a narrow waist. Above that the machinery was beautiful, like a superb pair of 150 h.p. Volvos. She was a brunette, I guessed about twenty-five, and the long black hair framed a sun-tanned face whose pert nose only emphasised the wide, peachy mouth and the big brown eyes. There was only one thing that spoiled the picture. He was tall, blond and ridiculously handsome, and what was worse, she was holding his hand.

'Good morning. Are you looking for someone?'

It was the girl who answered. 'You don't recognise me, Max?'

I squinted up into the sun and looked at them both.

'No. I can't honestly say I do. How about we introduce ourselves? If you step down there on to the seat, and then down here to the deck, you could sit down. Meanwhile . . .' I said, and I hauled myself up from the innards of the boat.

They sat very carefully, like two good children.

'I'm Max Farne. Welcome aboard.'

'And I'm Sally. I met you twice when you knew my sister Grace.'

And then the penny dropped. But there was only a fleeting likeness. Grace was pretty but this one was gorgeous. She sat unembarrassed as I looked her over again. She must be pretty used to it. And then she spoke again.

'And this is my brother Frank. He brought me down here to see you.'

And at that good news brother Frank seemed even more handsome than he had before.

'Of course. How is Grace?'

'She's fine. She sends you her love. She's married now. He's a solicitor.'

She paused to see what effect the news had. Grace and I had had almost fifteen months together. She'd been on the rebound from an advertising man. Before that she'd been a "model" in a Follies show. "Models" are the ones who are starkers but don't move. They've got more status than the strippers but they earn less dough. Gracie was a warm, laughing sort of girl, the kind that always gets cornered by married men. When she'd packed her bags to go after our time together nobody had got hurt and she was back on an even keel. I'd never have paired her with a solicitor, but I guess solicitors come in all shapes and sizes.

'That sounds great. She happy?'

'Oh, yes. But always says you made it all possible. She calls it the Max Farne rejuvenation cure.'

'And you were the little girl with the labrador at the cottage?'

For the first time, she smiled. 'So you do remember.'

'How about a drink. Tea – or coffee?'

'Can I talk to you first?'

'Sure. Let's go down in the saloon.'

We sat around the teak table. They were both a bit strung-up and, now I could see her face properly, I noticed the signs of strain.

'Right. Tell me.'

'It's about my baby.'

I hadn't noticed a wedding ring and as I sneaked a look at the long brown hands I saw why. There wasn't one. She waited for me to speak.

'Go on.'

'I'm not married, you know.'

And there's nothing much you can say to statements like that unless you're a writer for the *Sunday Times'* women's page.

'She's been kidnapped. Taken away.' And she waited for a comment.

'Have you told the police?'

She shook her head.

'No. We decided it was best not to. At least until we'd spoken to you.'

'I see. Tell me about it. When did it happen?'

'Two days ago.'

'What happened?'

'I just woke up that morning and the flat seemed specially quiet. I went to look in Rosie's room and she was gone. The bed was empty and her clothes had gone and . . .' The voice quavered and the tears that had been hanging on the rim of the gentle brown eyes just rolled down her cheeks. Slowly and separately till they stopped at the soft upper lip and hung like raindrops. '. . . There was a note.'

She opened the white linen bag and took out a folded sheet of paper and passed it across the table. It was a short note. Handwritten. It just said:

Sally,

Owing to your outrageous behaviour, I am leaving you. For her sake, I am taking Rosie so that she can be brought up properly. Perhaps in due course you can see her from time to time.

Jeremy

I looked up at her and the pretty face waited patiently for some new indignity to be heaped on her.

'And what's happened since?'

'Don't you want to know about the outrageous behaviour?'

'No. I don't believe that bit. It's a phoney excuse.'

She put her head down on her arms on the table and sobbed. Frank looked concerned and opened his mouth to speak. I put my finger to my lips and shook my head. He leaned back, looking unhappy, but he didn't speak. Then the wet face came up slowly.

'It hurt, that bit. It's so unfair.'

'Look, Sally. It doesn't matter a damn. If he'd had good grounds for doing what he did, he'd have talked it out with you or done it legally, not just sneak off. I'd guess he's left before. This wasn't the first time, was it?'

'No. He left me several times. Just went out and didn't come back. The first few times I was frantic, but he didn't take Rosie.

But the last time I didn't feel so broken up, I didn't rush about after him and eventually he phoned. After about six weeks. And he came back.'

'Is he married?'

She nodded. 'Yes. He's got two children.'

'So why haven't you been to the police?'

The girl sighed, breathing in with a shudder like babies do when they've cried too long.

'You take over, Frank.'

'Well, we had a meeting with George, Grace's husband, and he advised us against it. He said he'd explain the legal position to you if you would help Sally. He thinks we'd do better to find her and take her back. But he can't advise that officially, of course.'

'How old is the baby?'

'Two years.'

Sally shook her head. 'Two years and five weeks – six weeks, now.' And the tears came again.

'And what do you want me to do?'

Frank looked very young and not very hopeful.

'Sal wants to ask you to find Rosie and get her back.'

'Where does Grace's George practise?'

'His offices are in Holborn. He's junior partner in quite a big firm. But he's really a commercial lawyer, doesn't usually handle family things.'

'Have you got his phone number?'

'Yes. But he'll be at home now. It's Saturday.'

'The phone's up there on the chart table. Phone him and ask him if he'll see me in two hours' time at his offices. Between twelve and one, say.'

I could hear him talking and then he was back in the saloon.

'That's OK, Mr Farne. He'll see you then. He'll wait till you get there. Says don't rush.'

'What were you planning to do now?'

'Nothing, Mr Farne. Can we wait till you come back?'

'Sure. Take Sal for some lunch at the Yacht Club. It's alongside the chandlers' back up on the road past the boatyard. Tell them you're boat clients of mine.'

The streets around Staple Inn, Holborn, were almost empty and I parked the white MG near to the big ornamental iron gates. The outer door of the empty offices was open and a voice called from the stairs.

'Come on up, Mr Farne.'

George Pallant was a good deal older than I had expected. He must have been fifteen or twenty years older than Grace. He was wearing his office clothes and there was a touch of formality about his face. The handshake was firm and the smile was for real.

'Come in, Mr Farne. We shan't be interrupted on a Saturday.'

'It was good of you to meet me at such short notice.'

'Not at all. It's our thanks to you. Grace sent you her love. She's very, very worried about young Sally. We all appreciate any help you can give.'

He sat back and looked at me, and shifted his blotter slightly as he looked down at his desk.

'How much do you know?'

'I know Rosie's been taken by her father and that he left a note. That's about all.'

He nodded. 'Good. There's more to it than that, of course. Let's start with the young man. His name is Jeremy Martin. He's about thirty-four, thirty-five, something like that. His parents are very wealthy, and very influential, too. The father is an art dealer with galleries in London, Paris and New York. The boy hasn't done a real day's work in his life. Had a series of little sinecures from friends of the family. A couple of hours a day in a friend's gallery. Writing little pieces on art for moribund country papers, that sort of stuff. Has been perilously near to prison two or three times. Forged cheques, drunkenness and that sort of thing. A spoiled brat. A rascal. But like a good many of the type, plausible, good-looking, charming and utterly self-centred. When caught out they beg forgiveness and despise the weakness of those who forgive them. Unstable personalities who spread disaster on all who are unlucky enough to be influenced by them.'

He paused and tapped on the desk with a gilt letter-opener. 'A bit like the man you rescued my Grace from.' He smiled and all the hidden warmth behind the formality shone through. It was nicely done. He handed out the laurel wreath, showed that he knew, and made the nice point with 'my Grace'. I could see his attraction for her.

'Let's get to the present mess. Before I go into the legal aspects, can you tell me your feelings about their request for active help?'

'In principle I'll help, but I need to know more before I actually commit myself to anything.'

'Quite right. You realise that not even in these four walls can

177

I recommend or approve any particular course of action beyond the remedies the law provides?'

'I'd expect you to tell me if anything I had in mind was illegal.' I smiled. 'If I asked you.'

'We shall have to be very circumspect in our discussions, Mr Farne. What I would be mainly concerned with is that nobody should do anything that would put us in a bad light when we eventually get to court.'

'Unless we find Rosie it won't come to court.'

'In a way that's true. The court would be very reluctant to make an order that it had no power to enforce.'

'You mean if Rosie were taken overseas?'

'Exactly. And that is what we're all afraid of. Meantime, there is some moral support that I can give Sally that could help in your search. On Monday I shall make Rosie a Ward of Court. If we are very fortunate the judge might order that the little girl should be returned at once to her mother. He might even make a statement that he seeks the help of the public and the Press to that end.'

'Has anyone got any idea where Rosie might have been taken?'

'When Jeremy deserted Sally in the past, I suspect that other women were often involved. If he were foolish enough to involve Rosie with another woman, his case in court would be hopeless.'

'Don't courts always give custody to the mother?'

'Not these days, Mr Farne. They take a broader view. It would depend on the environment, characters and stability of the two parties. There's more to motherhood than mere procreation – and to fatherhood, too.'

'What about the boy's parents?'

'A good point. A good point. The reference to "outrageous behaviour" makes me suspect that he has had some sort of legal advice or warning, and that was put in to serve as an excuse. As far as I can understand, the parents are quite indifferent to their son. Their contact has been very spasmodic for some years. However, they have always adopted the attitude that young Sally led their innocent boy astray. It's a pack of nonsense and the reverse of the truth, but it serves their purpose. They have made a number of attempts to persuade Jeremy to return to his wife and children. A court would uphold that thinking, but in my opinion it was done for social reasons. They would rather have their black sheep appear to be seduced rather than have him regarded as a blackguard. They may have some part in this or they may get dragged into it if Jeremy

178

gets in a corner. Inadequate psychopaths can always write a good scenario for their misdeeds.'

'Why do you think he took Rosie? Is he all that fond of her?'

'I think he is fond of her. It wouldn't be fair to say otherwise. There will be some genuine affection for an attractive baby but I see the child's removal more as an insurance policy. He'd learned already that Sally was no longer so distressed on those times when he left. Unhappy, maybe, but no longer desperate and ill like she used to be. So if he bolts again she may not have him back. With little Rosie he's holding an insurance policy. I don't think he will have expected any legal action. He's arrogant enough to think that Sally would be at a disadvantage as an unmarried mother.'

'Has he supported Sally and the baby?'

'For short periods only. My wife makes her an allowance. And that brings me to another point. You buy and sell boats for a living, Mr Farne?'

'Yes. I deal in boats, deliver boats and buy and sell them.'

'You make a reasonable living?'

'Enough for me.'

'I gather from Grace that people have come to you for help on other occasions.'

'That's true.'

'And they paid you.'

'Sometimes. There are exceptions. This would be an exception.'

He shook his head and pursed his lips.

'No, Mr Farne. Grace sent Sally to you because she trusts you. Somebody would have been employed. Not that I see you as employed. Grace has her own money now. And I have here . . .' and he opened a drawer, '. . . a cheque for a thousand pounds. It comes through me solely because I am Sally's solicitor. And this makes you official. You are, in a sort of way, an officer of the court now.' And he passed the cheque over to me. I folded it up and put it in my jacket pocket.

'Can you give me the boy's parents' address?'

He nodded. 'Yes. I have that here with the phone number and a private detective's report on Jeremy on the last occasion he left Sally.'

He passed across a brown file and stood up.

'Will you have a drink with me?'

'With pleasure.'

He looked, for a moment, shy. 'My name's George. I think you're Max.'

We walked down to El Vino's and had a couple of drinks. When I was leaving I asked him, 'May I go with you on Monday when you make Rosie a Ward?'

'Of course. Let's meet at the Law Courts. On the corridor upstairs. It's probably Court 17. My clerk was across there this morning.'

I turned off the Chichester Road down the lane that leads to Lavant and parked the MG against the hedge. There were only two cigarettes left in the pack and I lit one. By the time you've got grey hair and you're in your fifties, you should have got past rushing into things. You shouldn't prefer living on a boat to living in a house, either. The motor vessel, *My Joanna*, was a thirty-four-foot Fjord. Fast, roomy and well fitted-out. And she was home. Some people put down my odd temperament to the years I spent in Special Operations Executive. They're wrong, but I don't know the real reason. Maybe it's the independence. The boat's paid for so I only really need living expenses and a bit of capital to finance the boat sales. But it's more than that. When I start up those two big Volvos I can be heading for Cannes, or Honfleur, or Santa Margherita, or Alexandria. I can buy and sell boats anywhere. And I've got enough in various banks to go at least ten years if I never make another penny. And that smooth white GRP hull and the shining mahogany and teak seem to attract pretty girls. Mainly what my mother used to call "the wrong sort of girls". They're the best of the lot. The wages of sin is a hell of a good time and I square things off with the good Lord in other ways. Like looking for lost babies.

The fifteen months with Grace Elizabeth Scully had been spent mainly in the Greek Islands. She'd finished up tanned and slim and, what's more important, she hadn't used those pretty green-blue capsules to get to sleep for over a year. When you've been really kicked in the teeth it takes at least a year to get back on the railway lines, and pretty Grace Elizabeth had taken a couple of months longer. I'd hired a car and driven her to Athens airport when she decided it was time to go home. And when she was carrying her bag across the tarmac she'd looked up, smiling, at the balcony and, as she waved, she shouted the only Greek she knew – '*Kala merasis*'. 'Good morning' in Greek may not be the most romantic farewell after fifteen months and when it's late in the afternoon, but she was back in the world again and that was all that mattered. I knew I'd miss that easy laugh and the lithe young body. Not that night, because there was Aliki at the coffee-bar, but on the long trip back to Chichester when the radar had been fixed.

And now there was Sally. With the big brown eyes, and the turned-up nose, and the soft, warm mouth. Ought to be married to a duke, or modelling bikinis, but right now just trying not to cry *all* the time. An unmarried mum whose life-belt had been stolen. And I wondered if I'd have been all this eager if the face hadn't been so lovely and the legs so long and shapely. I hope I would, because I've got a sneaking feeling that if I'd been a girl I'd surely have been an unmarried mum. It's that mixture of courage and stupidity that does it. Give us romantics a flag to wave and we'll go to war; give us a kind word and we'll have a baby.

I'd stopped to sort out what I was up to but I hadn't sorted out a thing, so I pressed the button and slid down the hill towards Chichester. When I got to Birdham Pool I parked the car and walked down the jetty to the pontoon labelled "P". The lights were on in the boat, shining through the orange curtains. And I stood for a few moments looking down Chichester channel. The sun was just touching the hills across the creek and the sea was calm like solid gold. The air was sultry and slightly dark as the summer breeze scoured the green-with-seaweed looks.

I wondered what the two inside had been doing. The two inside had been reduced to one, and she was asleep with her head on her arms on the saloon table. The dark eyelashes lay curved on the flushed cheeks and the fine black hair swept sideways from her head to reveal the neat ear and the slim, childlike neck with its pulse beating visibly as she breathed quickly and shallowly.

I laid out two mugs and switched on the kettle. When the tea was made I sat opposite the girl and drank it slowly. It was nearly an hour later when she awoke. If you're desperately unhappy you don't come back into the world all that easily and, even when she'd raised her head, the brown eyes stared at me for a long time before I registered. She seemed too tired to speak, she just stared at me as if she were hypnotised.

'Where's Frank, Sally?'

'He had . . . to go . . . Mr Farne . . . gone to meet his . . . his girl . . . at Heathrow.' The heavy lids were half-covering her eyes. I made her some coffee and, as she sipped it slowly, she seemed to revive a little.

'Did you see George, Mr Farne?'

'Yes, I did, Sally. Look. It's going to be all right. We're going to get Rosie back so don't worry. Try to relax just a little bit and then you can help us.'

The lips quivered. 'But she's such a little thing. She won't understand what's happened. She'll wonder where I am.'

'She'll be taken care of, Sally. Sure, she'll miss you, but try and remember this. This is done to make you unhappy. It's deliberate, and the last thing Jeremy wants is to keep the baby. If he thought you didn't give a damn, he wouldn't have done it. So your best way of fighting back is to be as calm as you can. You've got a whole army of people on your side. Leave it to them.'

The big brown eyes seemed more aware as she looked at my face.

'Did you love Grace, Mr Farne?'

I smiled back at her. 'You'd better call me Max. Love's a big word, Sal. Different things to different people. Grace needed loving so I loved her. And she gave me a lot of love back. But she's happy now with her George. And I've been happy too. Sometimes on my own, sometimes not.'

'Can I stay here tonight, Max? On the boat?'

It was like a small girl wanting the light left on. You just say yes. I gave her the for'ard bunk and, when she was asleep, I went up into the wheel-house and telephone enquiries got me George Pallant's number. I told him Sally was staying the night and that Frank was returning to Putney with his girlfriend. Some men would have been tempted to issue words of warning on the protection of pretty young girls. Tactfully maybe, but recognisably. But not George Pallant.

'Very sensible, Max. She must be worn out emotionally. Keep us in touch. I'll let Grace know. Get some sleep yourself.'

I phoned the Martins' number the next morning and it was answered immediately.

'Sir Clement Martin's residence.'

'Good morning. May I speak to Sir Clement?'

'I'm sorry but he's not in residence.'

'Can you tell me where he can be contacted?'

'I regret not, sir.'

'His club, perhaps?'

'Sir Clement is not a member of any club, sir.'

And the arrogant male voice didn't bother to hide its indifference.

They lived at Petersfield, which wasn't all that far from Chichester and, when Sally had pecked at a breakfast, I took her off in the car. It was a good sunny day and even if nothing came of the visit, the journey would occupy her mind.

Cheriton House was on the east side of the town. It was a long Elizabethan house, well cared for with wide lawns and masses of roses.

Some instinct made me send Sally back to the MG and I walked up the flagged drive and round to the massive oak porch. I rang the bell and waited. Then a blue-rinsed lady came from a greenhouse. She wore gardening gloves and carried a trug in which were laid roses, garden twine and a pair of secateurs. The dress was simple but must have cost a mint and I'd have guessed at Courrèges. It was one of those very smooth, well-preserved faces with the hair swept back in wings on each side and a brown chiffon scarf clamping a chignon. She was good-looking and, at fifty, must have been the envy of many women of thirty-five. There was the fixed, patient, all-for-the-effect smile of the handsome woman being bravely considerate to the peasants. This charming smile is even for the likes of you.

'Lady Martin?'

'Yes. My husband's not here, I'm afraid.'

'Could I speak to you for a moment or so?'

'I'd rather not on a Sunday, you know.'

'It's a family matter.'

And the eyes closed just enough to be noticed.

'I think that's unlikely, Mister er . . .'

'Farne. Max Farne, Lady Martin. It's about your grand-daughter.'

'My grand-daughter?' and it sounded like Lady Bracknell saying 'A handbag?' She was torn between mere escape and a need to know. I waited for her to say something more.

'What have the girls to do with you, Mr Farne?'

'Not the girls, Lady Martin. The baby – Rosie.'

She looked over my shoulder to check if we were alone, hesitated for a moment, and was lost.

'I'm afraid you're grossly mistaken. There is no Rosie in my family.'

'I mean your son's daughter, Lady Martin. His illegitimate daughter.'

At that she clutched the trug tightly and swept past. When she was still within ear-shot I said quite loudly, 'The baby he has kidnapped.'

She swung round immediately. Her face drawn and white.

'What on earth do you mean?'

'Just that. He took the baby while her mother was asleep. He also left her a note to say he'd done it.'

'Oh, my God. But where would the poor boy go?'

'I've no idea, Lady Martin. I suspect he will land up here before long. And he's not a poor boy. He's a married man who deserted his wife and children. He's aged thirty-five and he's taken the baby as a return ticket to the mother.'

'I shall consult our solicitor about your wild statements, Mr Farne. You will be hearing from him.'

'Don't bluff, Lady Martin. You don't even know my address. And you'd be very wise to get your solicitors to advise your son about the law on kidnapping.'

She shouted her anger. 'If you claim he's the father it can hardly be kidnapping.'

'Removal without the other parent's consent is kidnapping, Lady Martin. This is my card with my address. I suggest you advise your son to contact me at once if you hear from him.'

She wanted the dignity of refusing the card but she knew she needed the information. She took it, glanced at it, and laid it in the trug.

'I assume that the baby is not here, Lady Martin.'

'How ridiculous.'

And she swept in and the oak door slammed behind her.

We were only back at the boat for about ten minutes before the phone rang. It was Sir Clement, well beyond melting point.

'Farne?' He bellowed.

'Max Farne here.'

'I warn you, Farne, you'll be hearing from my solicitors. Upsetting my wife. Trespassing on my property. Slandering my son. This will cost you a pretty penny. What?'

I was always fascinated by men who actually did punctuate their sentences with "what". So I waited.

'D'you hear me?'

'Very plainly.'

'What's your answer, then?'

'What's the question?'.

'Damme I've just told you.'

'Sir Clement, your son Jeremy has committed a very serious

offence. I suggest you advise him to return the baby immediately. He is causing the mother acute distress.'

'Serve the silly bitch right, mucking up his marriage, making a mess of his life . . .'

I crashed down the phone as he was in full flood and prayed that his anger was as consuming as mine.

Sally sat patiently, waiting for me to explain what was going on. I gave her the short expurgated version.

'Those bastards are worried all right, Sally. They're going to think twice before they harbour him.'

'But they'll love little Rosie and that might tempt them to keep her.'

I looked at the pretty face and was sad for her innocence.

'Sal, you're beautiful and I could hug you right now.'

She smiled and it was the first time.

By the time Sally and I arrived at the Law Courts it was ten fifteen and George Pallant was waiting for us at the main entrance.

'Well, Rose Elizabeth is now a Ward of the High Court.'

'Didn't I have to be there?'

'No, it's not necessary. Anyone can make a minor a ward if they give satisfactory reasons. On this occasion there was no problem. Now let's walk back to my office and talk.'

When we were back at Staple Inn he was very formal again.

'What I propose doing, Sally, is to issue an ex-parte application for custody and care and control. That would not only make her legally yours to look after but it would make it a serious offence for her to be taken away from you again, or removed even now from the country.' He turned to me. 'The Wardship proceedings give just a little more authority to you, Mr Farne. In trying to find Rosie you are in a way assisting the Court.' His phone rang and he listened and nodded from time to time. 'Thank you, Charlie, we'll go over right away.' And he hung up.

'That was my clerk. The application will be heard on Thursday. You will have to be there, of course. And now we shall all go over to see Mr Lovegrove, the barrister who will be handling this for us.'

Mr Lovegrove's chambers looked prosperous and he got up from behind a massive desk when we were ushered in.

'Ah, Pallant. Sit yourselves down. I shan't take up too much of your time.'

'This is Miss Sally Scully, Mr Lovegrove, and this is Mr Farne, a close friend of the family. I mentioned him to you on the phone.'

Lovegrove nodded at Sally and gave me a sharp look. Then he leaned forward with his arms on the desk, looking very earnest and well-washed.

'Have you got the note, Miss Scully?'

He read it carefully then looked at Pallant.

'I think you're right, Pallant. The outrageous behaviour bit looks as though someone has put him up to that.' He turned to look at Sally.

'Is there anything at all you can think of, Miss Scully, that this comment could be based on? Some complaint of some kind? Trivial, maybe?'

'Not that I can think of. Certainly he never said anything.'

'Have you got a doctor?'

'Yes, but Rosie's never been ill.'

'I see. Has she had all her jabs and that sort of thing?'

'Yes, but that was at the clinic.'

'Ah, good. Pallant, perhaps you'd get a statement there for me?'

George Pallant reached for his briefcase and pulled out a file. Found two papers and passed them over.

'There are two copies there for you, Mr Lovegrove.'

Lovegrove was pleased. Sally might be a relative of Pallant, but the solicitor was doing his homework. And he'd done it before he had decided to go ahead legally. Lovegrove purred.

'Now tell me, Miss Scully, if the father wanted to make a condition of returning the infant that he came back himself, what would you feel?'

There was a long silence which Lovegrove eventually broke.

'Let me make clear that he would in no way be entitled to make such conditions, neither would the court entertain them for a moment. It is for my information in case the other side approached me.'

'Who's the other side?'

Lovegrove smiled. 'The baby's father or anyone acting on his behalf. This is an ex-parte application and that means that evidence is only given by one side – that's you. But the other side can always enter a defence or a counter-application which the court would hear.'

'No. I wouldn't have him back.'

Lovegrove nodded and shuffled a pile of briefs to one side.

186

'Now a couple of very personal questions, Miss Scully. Have you ever had treatment for a venereal disease or had an operation for an abortion?'

'No.'

'No to both questions?'

'Yes.'

'Have you ever been paid in any way – money or substantial gifts, for sexual intercourse?'

'No, never.'

'Right. I think that's all. But I'd like a word with you, Pallant, about the father if you'd care to settle your clients outside.'

We arranged to meet George at the coffee bar in the Strand. He seemed pleased when he joined us. Thought that everything was going according to plan. But the three of us were aware that none of this would get back the baby. It was good background stuff for the future but the principal party was missing.

It was time to get down to business and I asked her, 'What sort of places did Jeremy go to when he went off?'

'I think he generally stayed with other girls.'

'You know any of them?'

'There was a Marcia. Marcia Fellowes, and a Judy.' There was always a Judy.

'Where did they live?'

'Marcia lived on the King's Road near Royal Avenue, and Judy was in Fulham somewhere. A converted house on the Fulham Road next to a pub called the Horse and Groom. I've just remembered, her name was Farrow – Judy Farrow.'

'And where did you and Jeremy live?'

'Putney Park Road. Number thirty.'

'Have you got the key?'

She fiddled in the white bag and brought out a Yale key.

'Do you mind if I go there and look around?'

'No. Would you bring me some clothes?'

'Of course. Anything in particular?'

She shook her head and her mouth was trembling. George Pallant spoke up quickly.

'I'll take Sally to lunch and then back to the office. We'll meet there, Max, whenever you're finished.'

'Can I come back with you, Max, and stay on the boat?' The brown eyes were pleading and they didn't need to. I glanced at Pallant but his face was blank.

'We'll go back together, Sal. You make that your base till this is over.'

'I like the boat, Max. It's away from all this nastiness.'

'See you later.'

The flat was in one of those grim Victorian rows off Putney Hill. If they were in New York, Louis Auchincloss would make them sound interesting. But they weren't. They were built of those dull grey bricks that make it look as if it's raining even when it isn't.

There were four names on the small bell panel and one of them said: "Mr & Mrs Martin. 1st Floor". The door and stairway and corridor were all painted with that special brown paint recommended for HM Prisons. Reformers frequently say that young men should have to watch babies getting born before they start going round getting into mischief. This little dump should have been compulsory warning for randy romantics who whisper to pretty girls — 'We could manage, darling. All we should need would be a big bed and a frying pan.'

The door of the flat opened easily enough. There was a small living-room and a bedroom, and a bathroom without a bath. The baby's bedroom was on the far side of the living-room. The traditional Picasso print of Don Quixote was on the shelf over the gas fire and a couple of outdated *Cosmos* lay dog-eared by an armchair. The only room with any life was the baby's room. The walls were bedecked with colour pictures from magazines and there was a heap of cuddly toys beside the bed. The drawers of a small chest were all open, left from the swift collection of the baby's clothes. There was a plastic bath and bath-time toys and the curtains were lacy and feminine.

In the other room there was a ramshackle wardrobe and the only male clothing was a worn tweed sports jacket and a pair of suede boots. On a shelf was a row of photographs. Grace, George and a younger Sally with an elderly labrador standing outside a hotel. A glamorous portrait of Sally and half-a-dozen snaps of the baby. There was one photograph of a man I guessed was Jeremy. Good-looking, black wavy hair, big soulful eyes and a soft feminine mouth. A 1930s playboy. I could see the attraction. There was a silent desolation about the sitting-room. The air heavy with loneliness. Young Sally must have often sat here alone. Sad and solitary with no one to comfort her. I packed some clothes into a battered case. The ones who sneak out always take the best cases. I took three of the snaps of the baby and the photo of Jeremy.

We were back on the boat mid-evening. It had been a fine summer's day but we hadn't noticed. But now we sat on the aft-deck with long drinks and the breeze setting halyards and sheets flapping and clattering on the lines of moored sailing boats. There was plenty of work going on with varnish and paint pots, and children manoeuvring dinghies around the main pool. But the golden sunset didn't disguise the deep sighs of the girl who sat beside me thinking of her baby.

I rang George Pallant to see if he had an address for Jeremy Martin's wife. He had. It was in Richmond near the park. I left a note for Sally, who was still asleep when I left.

The house was about what I expected. A mock-Tudor detached house on a small estate of similar houses. A young woman was putting a couple of empty milk bottles on the porch as I got to the gate. As she straightened up she pushed back a long flow of blonde hair that in the old days would have been a Veronica Lake hair-do.

'Mrs Martin?'

'Yes,' she said hesitantly.

'My name's Max Farne. Could you spare me a few minutes?'

She looked as if she was wondering whether I was Jehovah's Witnesses or a canvasser for double-glazing.

'What is it you want?'

'I'd like your advice about your husband, Mrs Martin.'

She frowned. 'My advice? I don't understand.'

'Do you think we could talk inside . . . it's rather personal?'

Reluctantly she let me in, closed the door behind her and pointed to the front room. When we were both seated I said, 'Do you know about Sally Scully, Mrs Martin?'

'Is she the one he went off with?'

'Well – she's one of them.' I paused. 'He's the father of her baby.' I paused again. 'He's kidnapped the baby. I wondered if you knew where she might be.'

She shook her head slowly. 'Why on earth would he do that?'

'He'd walked out on her many times and he'd realised that he'd not be welcomed back this last time. So he took the baby as a kind of return ticket.'

'He's sick, that man. He really is.'

'Does he ever come back here?'

'He used to but I haven't seen him for at least three years. I wanted to divorce him and had ample grounds but his parents

189

begged me not to. They bought this house and set up a trust for me and the children on condition I didn't take him to court.'

'You mean on account of his adulteries?'

She shrugged. 'That and other things.'

'May I ask what other things?'

She was silent for several moments, then she said, 'It wouldn't be fair to say any more.'

'Do you think it's fair to snatch a baby away from its mother?'

She looked down to where her hand was plucking imaginary threads from her skirt. Then she looked up at me. 'What part do you have in this?'

'I'm a friend of the mother's family. They've asked me to find the baby. She's been made a Ward of Court. Technically it's very near to kidnapping. It will go to court next week and then it will be in the papers. But I'm scared of what might happen to the baby before then.'

'Do his parents know about this?'

'Yes. I told his mother myself.'

'What did she say?'

'His father threatened me on the phone. Said he'd take me to court.'

'What for?'

I smiled. 'Men like him only go for people they think can't defend themselves. He won't do anything.'

'That's what he did to me. He was scared of what would come out in court about Jeremy. He said he'd have me certified insane.' She shrugged. 'He said the psychiatrist would say I was incapable of caring properly for the children.'

'You said *the* psychiatrist. Have you ever been to a psychiatrist?'

'I went once because they said it would help Jeremy.'

'What happened?'

'Nothing much. He just asked me about Jeremy's behaviour. I never heard any more.'

'Was Jeremy having psychiatric treatment?'

'Yes. He was in analysis for over a year.'

'Did he tell you about it?'

'He said the man was a fool. He laughed about it. But I found a copy of a letter that the psychiatrist had sent to his parents. They were paying for the treatment.'

'What did it say?'

'It said he was a psychopathic personality. Entirely selfish and indifferent to the harm he did to other people. It was pretty bad.'

'Have you still got the copy?'

'No. I destroyed it. It sickened me.'

'Why did you marry him?'

She shrugged. 'I was young and stupid. He's very good-looking and was very charming.' She smiled wanly. 'He can be very charming when he wants to be.' She sighed. 'When he's just been caught out. Promises he'll never do whatever it was again. And does it again the next day. He has no conscience.'

'Would you be willing to say this in court?'

'Good God, no. I'd lose the house and the trust. I'd be finished. They'd see to that.'

'Who was the psychiatrist?'

'I'd need to look it up.'

'Would you do that? And his address?'

She was away for about five minutes and then she gave me a page from a small note-pad. It said: "David Jacobs, 24 Squires Lane, Croydon". I thanked her and left and walked back to the MG.

At the next public phone I called the boat but there was no reply, so I decided to have a look at the Squires Lane house.

It was a long drag across London and I parked the car well away from number twenty-four. Squires Lane may have once been a lane but now it was just another suburban road, a gently sloping hill lined with plane trees. The house itself was late-Victorian and although there was no brass plate at road level I could see one beside the front door of the house itself. I could see no signs of a security system but I wasn't equipped to do anything.

And although there were vague thoughts buzzing around at the back of my mind there was nothing I wanted to do at that particular moment.

It was a long trip back to the boat and when I got back I took Sally to the yacht club where there was a message for me from a man who'd looked over a thirty-two-foot Princess that I'd renovated completely. It was an old boat but in good condition and Princesses held their value. He wanted it and that gave me three thousand pounds profit for my Swiss bank account.

When we got back to the boat there was a message on the answering machine to phone George Pallant. It was bad news. He had been phoned at home that the other side were going to enter an appearance on Thursday to contest the custody of the baby. Pallant had the feeling that they were going to play dirty. But bad news sometimes helps you make up your mind.

The next morning I checked the psychiatrist's telephone number and called it every half-hour. An answering-machine message was all I got. And that suited me fine. I checked my small leather fold-up and the contents and then took Sally and the boat out as far as the harbour bar. It was a dangerous bar with shifting sands and changing currents and there was no point in taking any risks. I turned back and made for the lock into Birdham Pool and when I'd tied up I went across to the club to sign the papers and pick up the cheque for the Princess.

It was beginning to get dark as I headed for Midhurst and eventually the house in Squires Lane, Croydon. I left the MG on the dark forecourt of a closed Shell station, then walked to a phone-box and dialled the psychiatrist's number again. It was still the same message on the answerphone. I checked my watch. It was 1.45 a.m.

I walked up the hill to the house and then up the brick steps and round the side. There were no lights on in any of the rooms. Whoever had locked the backdoor had been careless and had left the key inside in the lock. I unravelled the soft leather pouch from my briefcase and took out a pair of hollow-nosed pliers. I squirted a few drops of Rust-free into the lock, waited for a couple of minutes and then slid the pliers in the key-hole to grip the key. It was an old-fashioned lock with heavy tumblers and it took four attempts before the key finally turned. As I turned the door-knob I held my breath and hoped that there were no bolts on the door. In fact there was one but it hadn't been pushed home properly and the door opened easily.

I shone my torch around a quite large old-fashioned kitchen with an Aga cooker. The cooker hot-plates were cold and I guessed that Mr Jacobs must be on holiday. The door to the hall was open and as I walked along the tiled hallway I saw what I was looking for. A door marked "Waiting-room". There was a receptionist's desk and four comfortable chairs and a door leading to an inner room. But the filing cabinets were here in the waiting-room. A line of grey metal cabinets with labels on the ends of the drawers. I found the one marked "M–O". There was the usual silly lock that held all three drawers. I slid in a feeler and turned it slowly. Two pushes and two turns and the lock was free. I thought at first that there was no file for Jeremy

Martin but it had just been filed carelessly out of order. I took
it to the secretary's desk and switched on the table light. There
were the notes on the sessions with Martin, correspondence with
his father, copies of billings for the treatment and one last letter
to old man Martin.

I found a pad and a Biro and made notes of a number of items
and I unclipped that final letter to his father and tucked it into
my pocket.

It was beginning to get light by the time I got back to the boat.
I set the alarm for 9 a.m. and slept.

George Pallant read the last page again, folded it over and handed
it back to me, leaning back in his chair, sighing as he folded his
hands and looked at me.

'Let's say I've never seen that letter.'

'Why? Surely, if they're playing dirty we should respond.'

'If I offered that in evidence you'd go to prison. Probably for
breaking and entering, and certainly for theft.'

'But it says quite plainly that he's mentally sick, a psychopathic
personality, a proven liar – even to his analyst. And a menace to
society.'

'It doesn't matter what it says. If I put that in evidence the
other side would slap an injunction or a writ on me in a couple
of hours.'

'So don't show it to them. Just use it in court.'

'It's called "discovering the evidence", Max. Any evidence you
want to bring up in court you have to show to the other side in
advance.'

'That's crazy.'

'No, it's not. It's the law. And there are good reasons for it.'

'So you don't want it?'

'I don't know what you're talking about, Max.'

'What are they saying about Sally?'

'They want to establish that she's irresponsible, incapable of
bringing up a child. That the baby should be in the care of
its grandparents – Sir Clement and Lady Martin. It's just a
mud-throwing operation.'

'And we're going to just let them get away with it?'

'Of course not. We shall fight it all the way.'

I looked at his face and I knew he was no longer sure that Sally
would get her baby back.

'Who's acting for them?'

'Parsons and Lane. Very prestigious.'

'Any indication of where young Rosie is?'

'Not exactly. The implication is that she's with them – the grandparents – but it doesn't say that.'

'Will they have to say where she is at the hearing?'

'Yes, if the judge requires it. We shall certainly insist on them revealing where she is.'

'And this is supposed to be justice?'

Pallant sighed. 'No, my dear Max. It's the law. And justice and the law are two different things.'

'And it helps a lot if you're stinking rich.'

For a moment or so Pallant didn't reply. Then he said, 'I hate having to admit it – but, yes – it helps a lot if you're stinking rich. Mainly because if you're rich and you lose and the other side gets costs it doesn't really matter. If you're poor it means disaster.'

'How about I take a trip down to their place at Petersfield and do a recce?'

'Anything like that, Max, and Sally's case would go down the drain.' He smiled wryly. 'SOE games wouldn't go down well in the Family Court.'

'Unless it's done by Jeremy Martin, of course.'

Pallant shrugged. 'The court won't like that, either.'

'I'll see you on Thursday then – at the courts.'

'OK.'

The crack about SOE "games" rankled. Special Operations Executive got results and to me it seemed high time that somebody did something more than writing letters and looking at law books. It was time that justice took over from the law if it left young scoundrels to snatch babies from their mothers and then claim the court's protection. But whatever I was going to do, I'd only got two days to do it in. Less than two days.

I hired a car in case they remembered the white MG and I trailed the Martins wherever they went. Shopping in Petersfield, to Chichester, and several trips to London and by the Thursday morning I knew where Rosie was and I knew that the Martins were all booked into the Savoy for Thursday and Friday nights.

I tried Judy Farrow first because I didn't know enough to find the one called Marcia. Like Sally had said, it was a Victorian house next to a pub and it had been crudely converted into bed-sitters. What estate agents call studios. Which meant that it was one big room and it was up to you what you did with it. It was a place for typists, secretaries and clerks who paid through the nose rather than face the commuter trains.

Judy Farrow's place was on the top floor and I could hear a radio as I pressed the bell. The radio stopped and the girl opened the door on the chain.

'Miss Farrow? Judy Farrow?'

'Who are you?'

'My name's Max Farne and I'm investigating the kidnapping of a baby.'

She frowned. 'Are you crazy or something? What the hell do you think I'd do with a baby?'

I smiled. 'The baby was kidnapped by a man named Martin. Jeremy Martin. I understand you knew him way back.'

For several moments she was silent and then she said, 'How did you know about me?'

'A girl named Sally Scully told me. It's her baby he's taken.'

'You're sure you're not kidding me?'

'Quite sure.'

She took off the chain and opened the door. 'Come in.'

We had talked for an hour and then I drove to the Hilton and booked myself in.

Pallant pointed to the chair facing his desk.

'What news have you got?'

'None. What's going to happen to Sally?'

'It depends on what the judge thinks of the two arguments.'

'And what do you think?'

Pallant took a deep breath and let it out slowly. 'I think we'll be very lucky if we get her the baby back.'

'Have you told her that?'

'No.'

'Why not?'

'I didn't have the heart to. And maybe I'm wrong. Maybe we'll win.'

'And his parents will get custody of the child?'

'I guess so.'

'Is that fair?'

'I told you, Max. This is about the law. Not fairness.'

'Not even justice?'

'I guess not.'

'What time does it start tomorrow?'

'He's got another case before ours. Noon or after the recess at two or two fifteen.'

I stood up. 'I'll see you there.'

Pallant nodded but he didn't speak. And even if he was Grace's husband, I knew he was a loser.

I paid through the nose for the ticket to *Phantom* and paid for it to be delivered at the Savoy.

She left the hotel at 7 p.m. and I went up to the Martins' floor half an hour later. I'd had a hunch that the ticket to the musical would be enough to get her out.

I knocked on the door of their suite and the old man opened the door. He'd never seen me and I said, 'Sir Clement Martin?'

'Who are you?'

'My name's Farne, Sir Clement, Max Farne.'

'Do I know you?'

'We've spoken on the phone.'

'What's it all about?'

'The court case. The baby.'

And the penny dropped. I put my foot against the door as he tried to close it, and leaned against it so that it pushed him aside as it opened. I closed it behind me and leaned back against it as he walked towards the phone on a trolley by an armchair.

'Don't use the phone, Sir Clement, or your name will be all over the papers tomorrow morning. They won't even have put the first edition to bed yet.'

He hesitated and then straightened up.

'I'll give you two minutes to get out and then I'll call the hotel security man.'

I held out the envelope. 'You should read this first, Sir Clement. Check what the newspapers will be phoning you about.'

I knew I'd scored a point when he walked across and held out his hand for the envelope. It wasn't sealed and he took out the contents and read the top page slowly. Read it again, and then leafed through the documents.

He looked at me with rage in his eyes. 'No court would accept this stuff. Not for a moment. And you'd go to jail for theft.'

'I didn't say it would be shown to the court. I said the newspapers. They'll love it. I gather you're not a popular man with the press.'

'Only the gutter press would take advantage of this . . . this filth.' He slapped it with the back of his free hand.

I smiled. 'You don't believe that, Sir Clement, any more than I do. Why don't we talk seriously?'

'About what?'

'About the baby.'

'Talk away.'

'How about we sit over at the table there?'

He shrugged and walked to the table, pulling out a chair and sitting down. I sat opposite him.

'Your son, Jeremy, Sir Clement. It's time he had a lesson in how to behave. To put it mildly, he's a social menace. Put more forcefully, the psychiatrist's confidential report makes clear that he's a psychopath.

'I don't think you read the last two or three pages, but they are a signed and notarised statement by a Miss Judy Farrow. Your son, while he was married, got Miss Farrow pregnant, having led her to believe he intended divorcing his wife and then marrying her. In fact, when she became pregnant he insisted she had an abortion. The hospital bill was paid by your son by cheque and there are photocopies attached to Miss Farrow's statement.

'That and the psychiatrist's report could well be considered by a court as evidence enough of your son's lack of responsibility.'

'He's a damn fool,' Sir Clement said quietly.

'You're right. But he's more than that. And this little caper was typical. For the sake of the baby's mother I'd be prepared to let you take responsibility for his behaviour in the future. Under certain conditions.'

'What conditions?' He lit a cigar and I knew that from now on it was just business.

'That the baby should be returned to the mother tonight and that you withdraw your son's application before it goes before the judge tomorrow.'

'This is blackmail, Farne. And you damn well know it.'

'You could be right. But that's how it is. It's your choice. I'm giving you the chance to avoid a major scandal and to do the right thing. You don't want that baby, Sir Clement. Neither does your son.'

'Why the hell did he do it? Tell me that.'

'He walked out on the mother many times. She was a fool, too. She loved him. But in the end he realised that she wasn't going to let him come back when his fling with some other girl was over. So he took the baby because he could use her as his passage back.' I paused. 'And, of course . . . because he likes hurting people.'

For a few moments he puffed on the cigar, his eyes on the envelope and its contents. Then he looked at me.

'Why tonight for the baby?'

'If she's back with the mother then the court case is never going to be heard. Both sides will withdraw their custody applications when the court clerks arrive tomorrow morning.'

He looked at me. 'The wife's grown very fond of the child, you know.'

I didn't reply and he stood up slowly. 'I'll tell the porter to get us a car. I'd better leave a note for my wife.'

'I can drive you down. Let's not have any more outsiders involved.'

He stubbed out his cigar. 'What d'you do for a living, Farne?'

'I buy and sell boats.'

'That make you a living?'

'Yes.'

He nodded and sighed. 'We'd better go then.'

It wasn't easy squeezing the portly knight into the passenger seat of the MG but it was a warm night and I put the hood down.

'We have to go on the Portsmouth Road,' he said.

'I know where your house is. The baby's there, isn't she?'

'Yes. There's a trained nanny looking after her.'

We didn't talk much on the journey. He asked a few questions about Sally and I told him as much as I thought was wise.

The arrogance had gone and I felt that he was glad it was all over. He'd taken his defeat quite well because I don't think his heart had been in it from the start. He was an arrogant man and he was going to have punishment enough dealing with that creep of a son.

The nanny was not too pleased at the baby being carted off in the middle of the night but the small bundle fitted nicely into what the MG specification referred to as the "courtesy seat" at the back.

I stopped the car in Petersfield and phoned Sally at Pallant's place where she was staying with Grace. There was a long silence when I told her the news and then I heard the phone clatter on a table or something and Pallant came on the line.

'I hope you haven't done anything stupid, Farne. I really do.'

'He phoned his lawyers while I was there. Both parties withdraw their applications first thing tomorrow morning. OK?'

'I guess so. Sally wants to speak to you again.'

I had nearly ten minutes of tears and laughing and I told her to hire a car and come straight down to the boat.

The baby's paraphernalia was in a canvas hold-all and I heated her a drink of milk. She looked none the worse for wear and tear, and I sent her to sleep with a Glenn Miller tape, and waited for Sally.

I've always reckoned that the only thing more beautiful than a boat was a pretty girl. But a pretty girl lying on a double bunk, asleep with her arm round a baby, is something special.

As I sat on the aft-deck with a drink, I looked at the stars and wondered if cleaning out the bilges didn't have some consolations after all.

When you first start in the writing game nobody, even you, knows whether you're going to make it. So publishers don't pay you much, which is understandable. They also insist that booksellers and the public won't stand for more than one book a year. So I started writing under another name – Richard Butler. I've no idea where I conjured that name from.

The Butler books were a change from the grimness of Moscow and the KGB. I love boats and I love Italians and Italy, especially the Costa Ligure and Santa Margharita. I wrote two of these stories – Where All the Girls are Sweeter *and* Italian Assets *– and they have been re-issued under my own name by New English Library.*

I'm fond of Max Farne, the character I created, and this short story was a chance to keep him alive and kicking.

As Time Goes By

She was wearing the Lanvin suit that she had bought in New York, a blouse from Fiorucci and shoes from a sale at Susan Dennis. She was dressed for battle but calm enough as the chat-show interviewer listened to last-minute instructions on her inter-com from the control gallery.

Then the floor director's hand went up for silence as he pushed down his outstretched fingers one by one to mark off the seconds before they were live.

'Good evening. My first guest tonight is Chantal Crawley – Business Woman of the Year, successful designer of furniture and everything that women use in a home.' The woman turned to look at her and Chantal was conscious of the TV camera moving in on her face.

'I'd like to ask you how you manage to look so beautiful and yet be the mother of two grown-up daughters, and a very successful business woman?'

Chantal smiled. 'Thanks for the commendation.' She paused. 'I started the business on very little capital because I believed that most household equipment was designed by men who never used the things they designed. The few things that were technically well-made were still badly styled. I thought that women deserved better.' She smiled. 'So I set about providing it for them.'

'You certainly did.' She paused. 'And, of course, made a fortune doing it.'

Chantal just smiled and waited and saw the confusion on the interviewer's face and the woman said, 'I gather you don't want to answer that question.'

'What was the question?'

Smiling toothily, the interviewer said, 'And then there's something else that maybe you prefer not to talk about . . . I'm referring to your service with Special Operations Executive in Occupied France during World War Two. You were parachuted behind the enemy lines?'

'Yes. I was.'

'Can you tell us something about your exploits in SOE?'

'I was working as the radio operator for a network in the Dordogne. There were no exploits.'

'But your network was attacked by the Gestapo and in the end you were captured and sent to a concentration camp.'

'Yes. But I was released by the US Army after a few months.'

'And you were only twenty-three years old then.'

'Twenty-three or twenty-four, I don't remember.'

'Well, back to kitchen sinks . . .'

It went on for another fifteen minutes. The rostrum camera showed pictures of the twins when they were about five and herself in FANY uniform. Some chatter about her French mother and finally her plans for the future, with fulsome thanks for coming on the programme.

Her PR people had heard on the grapevine that the interview was intended to show her in an unfavourable light, and she smiled amiably at the interviewer as the audience applauded and the commercial break came up.

The interviewer said, 'That was great. Thanks.' But the smile was a frosty, show-biz smile as the director's criticisms crackled away in her earphone. Chantal was accompanied by one of the assistants to where her car was parked. As she drove back to Chelsea she was amused at the failed attempt to cut her down to size. It was OK for women to be doctors or musicians but it was far from OK if they did better than men in a man's world. Especially if it made you rich and independent. Despite all the debates and promises, nothing had altered. It was just like those bastards at Baker Street after she'd come back from the camp. She could have forgiven them if they'd been sorry or comforting. But they'd been pompous and oafish. Admittedly they had no idea what had actually happened, but they had accepted that Peter was dead or missing without showing any regrets. And they had been only too ready to accept that she was responsible for the final chaos. They hadn't made a great song and dance about it. She was a woman and women panic. What else can you expect?

She had bitterly resented that snide 'And, of course, made a fortune doing it.' Going from one bank to another in 1948 had taught her a grim lesson. All she had wanted was two thousand pounds to get started. She had shown them her programme and cash-flow forecasts and even shown them drawings of her first three projects. One banker had looked at her drawings of a new style iron and seemed genuinely puzzled, and had said, 'But Mrs Crawley, there are several irons already on the market.' And one oaf had criticised the colour scheme of a hand-towel. How any man wearing an MCC tie could have the brass neck to comment on anything to do with colour schemes was beyond her.

In the end she had put an ad in the *Wall Street Journal* and had received two firm offers of all the capital she needed within two weeks. And along with the cash came some good advice and a lot of enthusiasm. Her two American partners got their investment money back nine months from the start of the operation. When retailers resisted her innovatory designs she opened a retail store in Mayfair herself. Two years later there were four more stores and twenty-five in-store concessions. When the City bankers came courting, it was a special pleasure to tell them to go to blazes. She had become even better known when she had been on a radio phone-in panel and a caller had asked her, 'What is the benefit of a lot of money?' and her instant reply had been that the real benefit of having a lot of money was 'the ability to tell bankers to get stuffed!'

Chantal knew that that wasn't the real benefit, but it expressed her attitude to people in authority. Particularly if they were men.

What she had disliked in the interview even more was the fishing expedition into her time in SOE. They had obviously done their research and, despite the Official Secrets Act, somebody had briefed them. If she had let them pursue it they would have tried to nail her as a successful businesswoman, but a broken reed when under pressure.

Oddly enough it was his birthday tonight and they always remembered it, she and the girls.

It was beginning to snow as she parked the car on double yellow lines in a turning off King's Road. 'Couldn't see any lines, m'lud, they must have been covered with snow.' She smiled. If you're a loner you have a tendency to talk to yourself, and a tendency to dramatise that makes you concoct scenarios and dialogue that turn a routine parking offence into Henry Fonda in *Twelve Angry Men*.

*

They never made the celebration of their father's birthday a sad occasion. She had told them, even when they were little, that he was a laughing kind of a man. Seldom serious and never solemn. They always finished with a plateful of meringues and eclairs.

As Christine took the last eclair, she said, 'What did he look like, Mama? Was he handsome?'

'He was about six foot. Black wavy hair, blue eyes, nice teeth and he seemed to be always grinning. Not handsome, but definitely attractive. Lots and lots of charm. Real charm, not phoney stuff.'

'Why don't we ever see his parents?'

She smiled. 'They didn't approve of me or our marriage. Come to think of it, nobody did.'

'Why not?'

'Well, his parents thought he was marrying beneath himself. The only son of a wealthy aristocratic family. Landowners, Lord Lieutenant of the County and all that sort of thing. And the top brass in SOE thought we were wildly irresponsible not only to marry in war-time but also when we were in enemy occupied territory.'

'Why didn't you wait until the war was over?'

She laughed. 'We were neither of us waiters. Anyway, if we'd waited we might not have had you two.'

'What happened to us when the Germans got you?'

'You were looked after by friends of ours. You've been with me to see them, way back. Remember the Dubois family? They took care of you for nearly a year.'

'Where were we born?'

'Just outside a town called Périgueux in the Dordogne. That's why you've got two passports.'

Joanna, who always thought long before she spoke, said, 'Do you feel lonely without him?'

'I felt very lonely at first but, as time goes by, you build up a life and everything just goes on.' She smiled. 'And I've always had you two.'

'But we were awful pests at times.'

'That's true. But you were a great comfort, too.'

'Were you brave when the war was on and you were in France?'

'No. I was scared stiff most of the time.'

'How did you get there?'

'I parachuted in.'

'And Daddy as well?'

'No. He went in a bit before me.'

'Did you love him at first sight?'

'No – I thought he was a spoilt brat. Rich, a red MG convertible, played polo and belonged to posh London clubs.'

'What made you change your mind?'

'Just time – and him, of course. He was always so cheerful. And he obviously liked me. We just fitted and got on well together.'

'Why haven't you ever married again?'

'Never found anyone I fancied that much.'

'But you've had lots of men who were obviously after you.'

'Most of them were after my money and the others weren't my style. Your father was a one-off. I've never met anybody else like him.'

Joanna said quietly, 'The perfect man.'

Chantal laughed. 'No. He certainly wasn't that. Far from it. But he was right for me. If you love someone you don't love them for a list of virtues. If they have failings you love them anyway.'

'I thought you told Marion Massey she ought to divorce Tom because he's a drunk.'

'No, I didn't. I said divorce him because she doesn't love him any more. That's different. And he doesn't love her either.'

'Why were you so cool with the TV woman?'

'Was I?'

Christine laughed. 'You know you were. I know that look of yours. A nice smile but eyes like lasers. You looked like that last night when that journalist phoned you.'

'Ah well, he deserved it.'

'Why?'

'Oh, the idiot wanted to come and interview me about what it was like in a concentration camp.'

'What *was* it like? You never talk about it.'

'Because nobody would understand what it was like if we talked for a hundred years. Now, it's time we were all thinking about bed.'

She wasn't sure that it was the first time she had seen him but it was the first time that she really noticed him. He was getting out of a Jeep, laughing at something one of the others had said. He was wearing his barathea, not battle-dress, and that was typical of the man. He said battle-dress was scruffy and there was no point in being scruffy if you didn't need to be. He'd glanced at her and grinned and waved his hand. He didn't know who the hell she was but she was pretty and that was enough. She checked with the others in her billet. He was Captain Peter Crawley, Intelligence Corps. And he was going to take over one of the networks in the Dordogne.

He had asked her for a dance at the Saturday night hop they had in the gym and he'd monopolised her for the rest of the evening. They'd gone into Southampton on Sunday and seen a re-run of Fred Astaire and Ginger Rogers in *Shall We Dance?*

She wasn't surprised when she'd been interviewed by a member of the training staff and asked if she felt ready to join a network as its radio operator. She'd said she was sure she was ready and, when he told her that she had been suggested by Captain Crawley for his network, she had smiled.

'Why the smile?'

'No particular reason. Just thinking of him makes me smile.'

He had seemed a little put out by the reply but he'd fixed an interview with Peter for the following day.

Peter had been more formal than she had expected. Going through her training record. Parachute jumps, unarmed combat, map-reading, small arms, radio maintenance and Morse, codes and radio procedures. And when that was through, those very blue eyes looking at her face.

'And what about you yourself? Do you want to go?'

'Of course I do!'

'Scared at all?'

'Yes, very.'

'What of?'

She shrugged. 'Scared of letting the side down.'

He nodded his head slowly as he looked at her. 'Good girl. It'll be about a month before we go and you can take a couple of weeks' leave.'

She had spent one week with him on his parents' vast estate. Replete, despite the war, with servants and gardeners. And no apparent shortage of petrol for several large cars and Peter's red MG.

Peter seemed a most unlikely product of his parents. The rather handsome but florid father. Polite to her because it was the correct thing to do with inferiors and servants. And then his mother. The adoring, aristocratic old bag. Asking who her parents were and what her father did. When she'd said he had a farm in Sussex she raised her eyebrows and said, 'A farm?' Like Lady Bracknell said 'A handbag?' in *The Importance of Being Earnest.* 'Ah yes . . .'

she said after a pause '. . . yes, we've got some farms on the estate.'

She had been slightly peeved that Peter hadn't stood up for her in one or two meal-time skirmishes with the old hag. When she told him so he'd laughed and said he hadn't noticed and, anyway, it didn't matter. She was like that. Nevertheless she had spent two almost sleepless nights beside herself with anger at some put-down in front of other people, her mind churning with the cutting replies that came with *l'esprit d'escalier*.

After all this, her week with her parents had seemed just a little bit boring. Listening to the same old village gossip, her father with the same old routines of milking and feeding pigs. But at least they were doing something useful for the war effort. Not just sitting on committees telling other people what to do.

It made no difference to her relationship with Peter, but it was the first stirrings in her mind of resentment for people who could decide your fate for you.

Chantal took the girls to the Special Forces Club for a snack and a drink on the Sunday following the TV interview.

As they sat at a table by the window looking out on to Herbert Crescent a few people came over and chatted to her, congratulating her on her TV appearance. But she noticed two who did no more than give her a brief nod from the far end of the bar. Mason and Fanshawe would have liked to cut her dead but they didn't have the guts to do it with others watching. They had both been desk officers at SOE's headquarters and had never been on active service, but that didn't stop them from passing judgment on her. She guessed that it was they who had refused permission when the French government had wanted to award her the Cross of the Liberation. The War Office had the final decision regarding the acceptance of foreign awards but she knew that it had never got that far. It had all ground to a halt on some desk at 64 Baker Street. But a representative of FFI had sent her an unofficial replica of the order, with its cross of Lorraine and green and black ribbon. It was in one of her jewel boxes at home.

It had been six weeks before she was dropped. Something to do with full moons and a decision to get Peter settled in before she arrived. They had gone to the cinema to see *Casablanca* the afternoon before he went out on a Lysander flight from the airfield at Tempsford.

The night she was dropped was a crisp, clean night at full moon and the reception committee and the lights had all been in place so there had been no problems. She was doubly welcome because she brought mail and a few much-needed medical supplies with her.

They had taken her to the stables of a farm the first night, and the next day she had cycled with Peter and one of the French resistance men to a garage in Chancelade about six kilometres west of Périgueux.

The garage was a sprawling cluster of old buildings that had once been a forge that employed two blacksmiths. But now it was a repair place for cars, trucks and agricultural vehicles run by a red-headed ex-army mechanic and two youths who helped him and looked after the solitary petrol pump. There was a row of what had been stables for visiting horses at the back of the house itself and the rear section of one of those was to be her living quarters and radio room. Her first transmission confirmed her own safe arrival and London responded with a brief five-letter acknowledgment.

In the first few months they had been concerned only with gathering information on the movement of German troops and identifying possible sabotage targets – mainly power supplies, bridges and railway marshalling yards.

By the following spring there were over fifty members of the network, all of them French except for her and Peter. They both spoke fluent French. Right from the French surrender the Dordogne had been substantially anti-Vichy and although people were glad that the war was over and had looked forward to the return of French soldiers, they were ready to resist the Germans secretly, and in a few cases, like the Abbé Sigala, quite openly.

There had been road-blocks and identity checks by the Germans but the network always got advance warning from one member or another of the network. There had been several successful drops of weapons, ammunition and plastic explosives, and a specialist weapons and explosives officer had come over for two weeks to show those concerned how to use the supplies. London seemed pleased with the build-up of information and the summer months had passed comparatively peacefully. London was still confirming that there was to be no activity against Germans or strategic targets until they were told.

It was August when she knew she was pregnant and Peter had arranged with the local priest for them to be married. The twins

had been born at the end of January and it was only then that
Peter had informed London of both events. At first London seemed
to have assumed that the signal was some sort of coded message
and asked for clarification. When they gave more details the reply
from London had been frosty and suggested that she and the
babies should be brought back. Forthwith, the signal said. But
Peter had just grinned and said, 'They'll probably send someone
over to persuade you to go back.'

'Do you think I should go?'

'It would be a lot safer for you. But it's up to you.'

'You won't order me to go back?'

'Good heavens, no. It's up to you. People are having babies
all over France so why shouldn't we? But I think we should put
them out of danger.'

'How?'

'Put them with a family until this lot is over and we can go
home.'

'Who've you got in mind?'

'The Dubois family at the farm at Merlande.'

'When?'

'In the next few days.'

'Why so soon?'

'Just a feeling in my bones.'

'About what?'

For a moment he hesitated, then he said, 'Remember the message
that they said I was to decode myself?'

'Yes.'

'It's not long to D-Day. And that means everything livens up.
Especially the Germans.'

As if they knew what was coming, the Germans had started
moving troops into the so-called Unoccupied Zone. And apart
from the Wehrmacht and the SS, the Gestapo had set up a unit
in Périgueux with a detachment in Brive to cover the rail junction
from Clermont-Ferrand to Bordeaux.

In the towns there were daily checks on papers with local units
of the Milice helping them, and there were road blocks on main
roads and checks on all passengers at the railway stations.

It was then that London called for action at last. They wanted
a list of suggested targets. Minor ones at first and then bigger and
more important targets once the Allies had landed.

In the middle of May they blew up the first bridges. One near

Brantôme and two railway bridges on the main line to the south. Then attacks on the telephone exchanges and electricity pylons. When the news came through of the landings in Normandy they reckoned it was just a question of time before it was all over. Informed guesses said it would be over by Christmas, but the unexpected German attack in the Ardennes had changed all that.

The pressure from the local Germans had increased and there had already been casualties in the network. But the turning point was when the SS division *Das Reich* had been ordered up from the south of France to join up with the German armies in northern France.

The network had been in action day and night, obstructing roads, blowing bridges and attacking isolated SS units. The Gestapo had closed in, torturing captured resistance workers to get information on the network, making more and more arrests.

After days constantly on the run, his face haggard with fatigue, Peter had been overwhelmed by what had happened to his men. She had sat holding his hand as his body trembled as if with an ague. He was no longer a self-confident, smiling man but a ghost of a man. A man at the end of his tether. When she asked about what had happened he seemed in another world, talking about his childhood, and then he seemed to be at Beaulieu giving instructions on stripping down a Bren gun.

She had slipped off to see Jean-Paul who had gone back with her and taken Peter away in the priest's car. Jean-Paul had been killed a month later but by then the network no longer existed. She had sent a signal to Baker Street saying that she could no longer carry on and two days later the Gestapo came for her. She wasn't interrogated because the Germans were in a hurry to get away to the north and she had been sent straight on to Ravensbrück.

When Fanshawe and Mason had de-briefed her she had only been back from the American military hospital for ten days. After a few perfunctory questions about her health, the questioning had started. It soon became obvious that they wanted to pin the blame for the network's collapse on either her or Peter. They had already told her that he was "missing, believed dead". And they implied that they were ready to accept that he was responsible for the final débâcle. The dead are always guilty.

She knew now how she should have dealt with them. Coolly

and destructively. But at the time she had screamed, shouted, cursed and wept with frustration and anger. Blaming them and their demands for the final weeks of the network's destruction.

They had sat there unmoved and when she had calmed down they ushered her out, wishing her well in her new life and confirming that she would get her widow's pension. She could remember standing in the street, her heart beating so fast that she thought she might collapse.

Seven years after the war was over she sat in the plane to Paris, trying not to let her mind go over all the possible scenarios for the hundredth time. And for the hundredth time she read the note that she had clasped in her hand. It gave an address in the Rue Antoine and four words: "Still love you. Peter."

She had been shocked when he opened the door. He looked just as he had looked the last time she had seen him at the garage in Chancelade. She'd worked out that he must be in his middle thirties but he looked like an old man. Grey haired, terribly thin and even those bright blue eyes looked pale and washed out. He was wearing a shabby tweed jacket, grey flannels and well-worn shoes.

They had talked all night and she could remember it now as if it had been only yesterday. And all the time she talked with him she knew she was talking to a different man. There was nothing she could say, no comfort she could offer that would change this shadow back to a laughing man again. That was all over. All she could do now was be some kind of ballast for what was left.

'What did they say when you told them I'd broken down and panicked?'

'Nothing, because I didn't tell them. I just told them that the last time I saw you, you were going off with Jean-Paul and I never saw you again.' She waited for a moment and then said, 'Just come back, Peter. Nobody knows anything. And what does it matter, anyway? You'd been under terrible pressure for weeks.'

He shook his head. '*You* know, Chantal. You saw me like that. I couldn't face them.'

'Couldn't face who, for God's sake?'

'The people at Baker Street. They'd rumble me. And my parents and my friends.'

'What have you been doing?'

He shrugged. 'Anything. Odd bits of translating. A tourist guide

211

around Paris. Cleaning. Washing-up in restaurants. You name it and I've done it.'

'Your parents would help. You could have a rest and get back to being your old self again.'

He shook his head as he looked at her face and said quietly, 'You know that ain't true. I've given up dreaming those kinds of dreams. This is me. I'm stuck with it.'

'I make good money from my business, I could keep you in funds. At least you wouldn't need to do anything you didn't like doing.'

'How are the girls?'

'They're fine, Pete.'

'Do they ever ask about me?'

'Yes. Frequently.'

'What did you tell them?'

'What I told everybody who asked. That you'd run a very successful network in the Dordogne and you were missing, believed killed in action.'

'Do they believe you?'

'Of course they do. It's true, anyway.'

'You'd better go.'

'Why did you send me the note?'

'I just wanted to see you again and say I was sorry.'

'You've no need to be sorry.'

'You ended up in a concentration camp.'

'And now I'm fit and well again. So what?'

'If I hadn't lost my nerve at the end I'd have saved a lot of people's lives and a lot of suffering.'

'No man can take on a chunk of the German Army and expect to win!'

'I'm ashamed, girl! I'll always be ashamed. And all these years I've remembered something you said when I interviewed you.'

'What was that?'

'I asked you if you were scared and when you said yes I asked you what you were scared of. And you said you were scared of letting the side down.' He sighed. 'It was me who let the side down. I ran away and you went in the camp. And some got killed.' He shook his head angrily. 'What a son, what a husband, what a father.'

As she sat looking at him she knew that there was no point in reasoning or arguing with him. He had lived this role for seven years and nothing would change him now.

She had asked him if he would like to see her again and he'd shrugged and said it was up to her. Every year since that meeting she had taken a week off and flown to Paris. She told nobody, not even the girls, what she was doing or where she was going. Booking her own flight and making her own arrangements. She guessed he was unaware of the significance of the time she chose which was always their wedding anniversary.

It was two weeks after her TV appearance when she took the call in her office.

'Hello, Chantal Crawley here. Who is it?'

'My name's Bruce Knight, Mrs Crawley, I'd very much like to come and talk with you.'

'All arrangements for interviews are done through my PR officer. I'm sorry.'

'You don't remember my name?'

'I'm afraid not.'

'I was OC Training at Beaulieu a long time ago.'

'You were Major Knight?'

'That's right.' He laughed. 'The fat one.'

'Why did you want to see me?'

'I'd rather not talk on the 'phone. Perhaps I could suggest we had a drink at the club, Special Forces Club. I know you're a member.'

'When?'

'Would six this evening suit you?'

'All right, but I can't stay long.'

'I'll look forward to seeing you.'

And he hung up.

He had ordered the club red and asked if she minded if he smoked. When she said no he'd offered her a cigarette, and she got the impression that the ritual was because he wasn't sure how to broach whatever he was going to say. When the cigarette was lit he closed his lighter, put it beside the cigarette pack on the table and then looked at her.

'Would you mind very much telling me when you last saw Peter?'

'I don't remember the date.'

He smiled briefly. 'I meant the place and the circumstances.'

'It was in a village near Périgueux. He was going off on an operation with one of his men. Jean-Paul.'

213

Knight looked at her and said, 'You're a very good wife and a very nice lady. And I've got great respect for you.'

'What does that mean?'

'I was in Paris for a couple of days to see my married daughter who lives there.' He paused and looked at her face. 'And I met an old friend. I guess you know who I mean.'

'I've no idea,' she said very quietly.

'I've got an awful feeling that there's something you don't know.'

'And what's that?'

'My daughter is a consultant at a hospital. He was a patient under her care.'

'What's wrong with him?'

'I'm afraid he's dead. That's why I contacted you.'

'What happened?'

'Nothing. He was in very bad shape. Pneumonia and a bronchial complication. He might just have pulled through if he'd tried. But he didn't try. He'd had enough of this world.' He sighed. 'I can understand that and I'm sure you can, too.'

She nodded her head slowly. 'Thank you for telling me.' She paused. 'What a waste. What a terrible waste.'

'That wasn't the only reason why I wanted to see you.'

'Go on.'

'He told me all about what went on in those last days and he insisted on giving me a written account and asked me to pass it on to the War Office. It's notarised and I've got it in my pocket now.' He looked at her intently. 'What should I do with it?'

'Give it to me.'

'And what will you do with it?'

'I shall burn it without reading it.'

He reached inside his jacket, took out an envelope and handed it to her. She slipped it into her handbag.

He said, 'I understand that Baker Street were not very understanding when you came back from the camp.'

'It's a long, long time ago.'

'But it would be tempting to show them how wrong they were about you, wouldn't it?'

'Not the slightest temptation, I assure you.'

'Why not?'

'I'd be paying with other people's blood. Other people's lives. Sacrificing a father, a much-loved son and a very charming man for the sake of saying my two penn'orth to a couple of old women

214

dressed as men, who never ran a greater risk than salmonella poisoning at some posh hotel in war-time London.'

Knight smiled. 'Peter pulled an awful lot of strings to get you on his team. He was a good picker, that man of yours.'

'Actually, he was very brave, very keen and very competent. They just ran down his batteries until there was nothing left.' And Knight noticed that for the first time there were tears at the edges of her eyes.

She had found out later that it wasn't just Bruce Knight but Sir Malcolm Bruce-Knight, ex-SOE and a member of the Royal Household. Five months later, on January 1st, Mrs Chantal Crawley became Dame Chantal Crawley in the New Year's Honours List. For services to industry.

'As Time Goes By' *was first published by* Woman and Home *in 1988. As you can tell from this story I'm a great admirer of the SOE girls.*